The Book on

From Hello to Hired

Hire Great Staff an

Business

With a foreword by Raymond Aaron, *New York Times* best-selling author, www.UltimateAuthorBootcamp.com

Reach Carole on 0044 (0) 845 124 0845, carole@thebookonrecruitment.com,

Twitter @CaroleFossey, http://uk.linkedin.com/in/carolefossey

For your bonus materials go to www.thebookonrecruitment.com and enter the code BOR1.

Table of Contents

Dedication and Thanks

Many people have helped me write this book – from my boss Rachel in a previous life, who first asked me to devise a new recruitment process for the company I worked for, to every single one of my high-level clients with whom we have used, developed and added to this process – thanks to all of you.

It goes without saying, of course, that without the support of my family – my husband Pierre and my kids Phoebe and Guillaume -- this book would have been harder to write. I know my children already understand that if you want something and are prepared to put the necessary action in, you can achieve whatever you can dare to dream. Thanks for all the childcare support to my long suffering mum, Judy, and to my brother Jon for keeping the business ticking over while I play, and just for being you to my big bro, David.

The actual structure and writing of this book began at a weekend seminar run by the wonderful Peter Thomson (www.peterthomson.com) – thanks for that creative energy, Peter; it started my journey. I was stuck on the book title and the (now) wonderful subtitle – "From Hello to Hired…" was dreamed up by a team of people directed and inspired by Peter.

The successful implementation and ultimate publishing of this book has been largely due to fantastic input and direction from *New York Times* best-selling author and friend, the incredible Raymond Aaron who, through his own hard work, passion and the making of many errors, decided to pass on his massive knowledge to other budding authors. Without his input I doubt the book would have been published any time this decade. Thank you so much, Raymond.

Thanks to David Walton – my long-time friend, employment partner at Gorvins Solicitors in Stockport (www.gorvins.com), and font of all knowledge regarding employment law in the UK. How long did we talk about this? And now it's finally here. You're a star!

There are some other people who have helped with this book without even knowing they did. There have been a lot of Michaels in my life, from my first boyfriend at sixteen, to my Uncle Michael (James Michael May), who was employed in one of the most dangerous and awe-inspiring jobs one can do – a firefighter.

There is Michael Heppell, who wrote the fantastic *Brilliant* books, who I first met at a Junior Chamber event in the early 90's and who I always find inspirational. My interest in writing a business book was piqued by reading "How to be Brilliant," which I highly recommend you read.

And there is also Michael Gerber, author of the *E-Myth* books, essential reading for *all* small businesses - whom I have heard speak many times and had the privilege of spending the weekend with back in 2006 (at a seminar, people!). This was a difficult time for me as it was just a few weeks before my dad passed over. Michael still managed to inspire me and give me some hope for the future in what were dark days for me. Dreaming of my future and of writing the book I had often thought about gave me something positive to focus on at that time.

Which brings me to the most important Michael of all – my dad, Paul Michael Fossey. You never let anything stand in your way, Dad. You were and are still the bravest man that I know, and the most inspirational. One day I will tell your story and the world will benefit from it. I miss you.

So, my Michael -- all my Michaels -- thanks for being in my life, for your inspiration, your support, your love and your encouragement, and occasionally for being a total pain in the ass. You are all responsible in some way for this book – whether you know it or not. I hope you're proud.

Foreword

Do you want to grow your business? Do you need to hire staff? Are you scared to death of getting it wrong?

Most business owners I know have one thing in common. They are all petrified at the thought of hiring staff and getting it wrong. After all, there are so many ways in which you can mess up! Personally, I love hiring staff, but I always worry about getting the right person into my business – or more accurately – about getting the wrong person.

So – I was delighted when I met Carole Fossey at an event in London, where I was speaking about my personal journey and the benefits and joys of being a published author. She spoke to me after the event about her passion for helping small businesses get the recruitment process right, and her desire to turn her client training course entitled "More Than a Gut Feeling" into a book and thereby reach and help many more people.

Carole has had a massively successful career in sales and recruitment for some of the biggest names in the UK – British Telecom, Yellow Pages, Marks & Spencer, and The S3 Group. Since early 2001, Carole has been running her own businesses and helping people throughout the UK, Europe and the US to get the recruitment process right. She has worked with huge international companies – and many smaller owner-managed businesses – and been instrumental in helping them grow.

Carole is a motivating, engaging and passionate person and it quickly became apparent to me that she knew exactly what she was talking about, and her message was one of vital importance to small and larger businesses.

I was so inspired I just had to help. And I was humbled when she took my suggestion to turn her title into her subtitle and renamed her book "The Book on Recruitment...From Hello to Hired, How to Find and Hire Great People and Grow Your Small Business." In my opinion, when someone is good at something, you can say they "wrote the book" on it.

Carole is not just good at recruitment – she is great at it. And more than that: she is great at breaking the process down into a simple to follow process that anyone can put in place.

I am so happy that you are reading this book because I know it truly will help you decide what you really need in your business and walk you through, step by step, each part of the process that you *must* follow when hiring. If you follow the steps given, you will be a thousand times more likely to get it right.

One point that really struck me was where Carole explains that most people start the recruitment process at the wrong place – the Job Specification. That made me sit up and take notice. Practically everyone I know does exactly that! But of course, it made perfect sense when she explained that in order to identify the ideal person for your business, you need to know what your business vision and values are, what its brand is (something I am very passionate about) and who its customers are. Only by identifying these things can you hope to put together a Job and Person Specification that matches your business and will result in a successful hire for the long term.

As Carole points out, most hiring processes in small businesses come up against three main problems: You are short of cash. You are short of time. Or no one ever taught you how to do it properly. Or all three!

With Carole's book, you have the benefit of an expert in her field holding your hand and teaching you everything you need to know.

That's why you should read this book from cover to cover.

Happy Hiring!

Raymond Aaron, *New York Times* Bestselling Author

www.UltimateAuthorBootcamp.com

Introduction

As you are reading this book I am going to assume you have either made one of the ten most common mistakes in hiring someone (which we will be looking at in more detail in Chapters 8 and 9), or are considering hiring someone for the first time and want to make sure you avoid those mistakes.

Before we move on to looking at those mistakes and how you can avoid them, I'd like to reassure you that whatever mistakes you have made - or are concerned about making - when hiring staff, please don't worry - thousands of other business owners and managers have made them before. You are not alone!

However, once you have read this book and put into practice the advice contained in it, you never need to fall into those traps again.

Perhaps you are the owner of a small business and need to recruit staff, possibly for the first time ever. Like most small business owners, you're passionate about your business and want to see it grow and therefore intend to do everything possible to make sure that you make the right decisions when it comes to the matter of hiring staff.

Or perhaps you are a manager in someone else's business and you have been asked to get involved in hiring the staff member.

In either case, the vast majority of managers and business owners have never been trained how to hire new staff, the most important of all management responsibilities.

So, congratulations. By creating the time to read this book, you are already ahead of the game. You are someone who cares about educating yourself and learning the skills you need to be the best you can be.

Just a quick word about me and why I am writing this book: I have been in sales, sales management and recruitment for many years. It has become apparent to me that the single most important factor in the success of the team or a business is the quality of its staff. I have seen, and made, many mistakes over the years when hiring staff. Taking on the wrong people in a business is always a problem - but in a small business it can be a disaster.

Let me tell you a story. It's a scary story, so you may want to turn on the lights and lock the doors.

Once upon a time there was a woman. Let's call her Helen. Helen was a hairdresser, a very good hairdresser. All her customers loved her and often told her that should she ever open her own salon, they would come with her. One day she decided to do just that.

She worked day and night six or seven days a week for over twelve months and her business began to do really well. It grew to the point where she took on another hairdresser, and then a short time after that they decided they needed extra help on a Saturday.

So they advertised locally and started to interview the people who applied. Eventually they found the person they wanted and everyone was happy. Or so they thought.

One night, Helen went home after a long day to find a letter. It was a solicitor's letter and it said that she was being sued for £36,000 for racial discrimination in an interview.

Our hairdresser was distraught. She had no idea what the letter was referring to. She didn't consider herself to be in any way racist and could not remember having made any comments which could have been interpreted as such in any of the interviews.

It turns out the applicant in question was a Muslim who wore a headscarf due to her beliefs and wouldn't take it off at any time in public. The hairdressing salon was an alternative salon, and like most hairdressers do, Helen wanted to showcase the hair of her employees as part of their marketing. I don't know about you - but I wouldn't want a hairdresser with terrible hair - or no hair on show - doing my hair; it's like selling Audis but driving a BMW.

The good news for the salon owner in this case is that the claimant did not win her claim of direct discrimination. But the bad news is that the tribunal awarded £4,000 for her "hurt feelings." You have to cut a lot of hair to earn £4,000 - it might be enough to put a small salon out of business.

There are other relevant points in this case, not least of which was that the claimant had been turned down by over twenty-five other salons for a job. Perhaps none of them were honest enough to admit the headscarf was a factor in their decision; perhaps they were more aware of the legal pitfalls.

This case shows the absolute necessity of having a proper interview process in place to protect you and to protect your business. It is unclear how much of a process Helen had in place, but it is likely there wasn't a process.

It is essential that the interview process is laid out in advance; that the core questions (those that directly impact the hiring decision) are laid out in advance; that all answers to questions are written down and kept and that all applicants are informed in writing that they are not suitable. It is especially important that you know how employment law impacts the hiring process.

If this sort of process had been in place, it is unlikely that the case would have progressed at all, let alone ended as it did. A costly mistake.

Like Helen, most small business owners launch into the business of hiring staff without any idea what kind of process they need in place or how to protect themselves from falling foul of the law. They don't know how to identify what they want, or interview properly.

That is the reason for this book.

For many years I have been training small business owners and managers like you to follow my Intelligent Behavioural Interviewing system for employing staff. This is not a quick fix. People come on my training course "More Than a Gut Feeling" and spend a day with me going through the specifics of their businesses and putting together a specific interviewing process for hiring their next employee. They put a minimum of a day of their valuable time into it to ensure they are giving themselves the best chance of getting it right.

I have to be up front with you and say to you that you will need to put some time into not just reading the book, but into putting into practice the process itself. But the good news is that this is a proven process and it will help you hire the right people and keep you on the right side of the law.

Employment law in the UK changes constantly – and the book will be legally correct as we go to press. For subsequent updates see the bonus material at the back. For readers outside the UK, please be aware that employment laws are different in every country – make sure you know what they are in your country before hiring staff.

Hiring someone should not be a one-off activity which is unrelated to anything else, but should be integrated into the core of the business, as we will discover in Chapter 2.

This book is not a book on interviewing, although we will cover interviewing and great interviewing tips in later chapter. This is a book about growing your business.

In order to take on the right members of staff for your business or your team, you need to understand what the vision and values of your businesses are. You need to know the following:

- Where you want to be in five years' time.
- Your customer base and how you want to interact with them.

- The service or product ranges you are offering and what level of quality you wish to maintain.
- What people love about your business and what they don't like so much.
- An idea of what your brand is and what it stands for.
- And crucially, what is it about your business that would make someone want to work for you?

Will work our way through all that in Chapter 2.

So if this is not a book about hiring staff, what is it about?

It's a book about growing your business and achieving the highest levels of success. In most businesses, a large part of that will be caused by hiring the right staff, and therefore, in Chapters 2 to 10, we will be looking at how to decide what you need. Once you are clear on that, we will talk about creating the perfect job and person spec and examine the most effective ways to find the staff that you want. In Chapter 4 you will learn about the magic 5-8: the core competencies that you need your next member of staff to have.

After all of those steps, we can then look at interviewing techniques, how to plan the perfect interview, and some dos and don'ts from the industry's top experts. We will also look at the ten most common mistakes businesses make when hiring staff.

Finally, we will look at foolproof decision-making. During and at the end of the book I'll detail for you a website where you can go and download essential forms that you need to help you with this process, and some other extra bonus material.

By using the process outlined in this book you will find you can sleep better at night, knowing that you have in your toolkit a tried, tested and proven method for interviewing and hiring the right people for your business.

Disclaimer

As with everything that involves people, no system can be 100% foolproof. "There is nowt as queer as folk," as the old saying goes, and that is certainly true when recruiting staff. However, with the proper process in place, you can be confident that you're doing everything that you can to cover yourself legally as well as conduct a meaningful recruitment process that will give you the results you want.

Chapter 1 – Before What, Why?

It is important before looking at the "what" to look at the "why." Why do so many people make bad hiring decisions?

The Three Biggest Reasons Why it Goes Wrong:

1. They are in a hurry.

2. They are short of cash.

3. No one ever told them how to do it properly.

Let's take these one at a time.

1.Didn't You Mother Ever Tell You, "More Haste, Less Speed"?

Mine did - but that doesn't always stop you, does it?

You know what it's like when you're busy - there is always too much to do - and taking time out to plan what might happen and what you might do about it if it does is not high on your priority list.

So what happens?

One day you come into work and your best salesperson/your PA/your sole IT person in the business resigns. You spend all morning trying to persuade them to stay - perhaps chucking more money at them, promising promotion, etc. Sometimes that works, but invariably only short term.

Mostly it doesn't.

So - you are in a mess. You rush it. You take the first person that comes along (probably through a recommendation or someone you know) that looks like they can do the job.

And then you breathe a huge sigh of relief because you have solved the problem. Haven't you?

Probably not.

In a small percentage of cases you might fall lucky and by accident have appointed the perfect person.

But in the real world, what generally happens is that three weeks or three months later, you realise that the person you hired is not up to the job, or they don't fit into the culture, or they don't have the skills you actually needed if you had stopped for a minute to breathe in the mad rush of solving the problem.

2. Cash Strapped?

Needing to hire someone always comes at the most inconvenient time - doesn't it?

If only you had the cash to use an agency, or put a great ad in the local paper/trade press to get to the right candidate pool.

Unfortunately, the taxman wants his money/the Vat is due/you just spent your spare cash on offices, marketing, a new car...

So you go for the cheaper option. Word of mouth. That's good, right? People who know you wouldn't recommend someone to you if they weren't right for your business, would they?

Now, don't get me wrong: word of mouth can produce some of the best people you will ever hire.

It *can*, I said. But not always.

And if you use word of mouth solely because it's cheap, guess what often happens? Yep - you get what you paid for. The cheap option not necessarily the best.

3. You Have Had No Recruitment/HR and/or Management Training

It isn't surprising.

Some people who run their own business may have had some management training. Many won't have. And the vast majority will never have had any recruitment or HR training.

In a small company the managers won't have had that training themselves and therefore can't pass it on.

In a bigger company, often there is an HR department, and therefore there is seen to be no need to train managers in these skills. Big mistake.

Very few people running their own business or running departments for someone else have the skills needed to avoid all the pitfalls of the minefield that is recruitment.

Given one or all of the above factors, it is hardly surprising that so many people get recruitment so wrong.

Don't worry though; there are things you can do to minimise your risk.

Chapter 2 - Where Do I Begin?

1. Deciding What You Want

This is actually the easy part. Most companies when hiring start with the job spec. That is entirely the wrong place to start and only one third of the three ingredients needed.

Later in this chapter we will look at creating the perfect job spec and creating the perfect person spec.

Before you can decide on either of those, you need to understand your business and how your business will develop.

Let's look at a client of mine. This client was growing rapidly and decided that they needed someone to help with the admin who could also do bookkeeping, and because they have a lot of French customers, they also needed to speak French. Unsurprisingly, they were finding it difficult to find somebody with all the skills they needed at a salary they could budget for.

When I discussed with them their longer term plans for the business, they told me that within six months they planned to take on a full-time finance person to do the invoicing, credit control, bookkeeping, prepare the VAT returns, etc.

I suggested to them that they outsource their bookkeeping to their accountants or a local bookkeeping company for six months until they were ready to bring it back in-house.

They also told me that within twelve months it was quite possible that they would need two administrators because of the projected sales forecasts and the admin support the sales team would need. It transpired that one of the directors who was office-based was fluent in French.

Therefore, we helped them to rewrite their job and person spec, focusing on a more senior administrator or possibly a PA who could manage a more junior member of the admin team. French language skills were a desirable rather than an essential skill on this new spec. In this way, they were able to find someone within their budget, with cash to spare, which paid for the additional bookkeeping services required.

This client could have wasted many weeks trying to find someone who could do everything they thought they needed.

They may or may not have found that person. Even if they had, they probably would have had to pay a far higher salary than they wanted to or had the budget for. Also, when the plans of the business came to fruition (regarding hiring someone to do the finance and the more junior administrator role), unless they were aware of that within their hiring process and hired someone with the right competencies to manage a more junior member of staff, they would have found themselves having to repeat the process six months down the line.

Equally, if they had hired someone with bookkeeping skills and then taken that part of the job away from them in six months time, then it is likely that member of staff would no longer be happy with their role and would leave.

So when considering what it is you *think* you want a new employee to be able to do, look at the business as it is now and as it will be and hire somebody who has the skills and experience you require them to have in twelve months' time as well as on day one.

2. Deciding What You Need

Following on from what we have just discussed, understanding where the business is and where it will be is the first step. Deciding what you really want and need your employees to do, bearing in mind where the business is now and where it will be, is the second step.

Deciding what you need - rather than what you want - really gets you focused.

In addition to this, there is an additional factor to take into consideration when you are replacing a member of staff that has left. It is crucial to decide whether you are trying to replace the person who joined or the person who left.

Let me explain what I mean by that.

One growing software development company who I recently worked with was looking for the impossible. They were looking to replace someone who had left at the salary that person was paid when they joined. Not only had salaries moved on and upwards during that time, but the person who joined was not the person who left.

The person who joined four years previously was a junior developer. They had some skills in an Internet development language – PHP - and whilst employed by my client they had learnt .Net and other Internet development languages. They had also learnt how to write script for various databases, and during that four-year period their salary had gone up three times. The company wanted to employ somebody with all the skills of the person who had left, but at the salary of the person who joined.

The owner of the company was too busy trying to sort out the problem of hiring to sit down and really think about how unrealistic this was. He hadn’t even recognised that this was what he was trying to do until we talked about it. He then realised that what he wanted was not feasible. So he sat down with his development team leader and they had a conversation in which they decided what they really needed.

Due to the amount of work that they had on at that time they decided they didn't have time to train somebody junior and bring them up to speed.

Therefore, what they needed to do was pay more than they had been paying the person who left in order to attract someone with that person's skills to fill the gap. This is a factor that you always need to think about when hiring. Do you have the time to train? If not, expect to pay more for someone with the skills you need who can hit the ground running.

Newsflash! Most people who leave companies go to other companies where they will be doing the same job but be paid more money for it. Even though this member of staff's salary had increased annually, it had not kept pace with the market rate. Therefore, that employee moved to another company that paid them £5000 per annum more. My client had to be realistic and increase the salary not just to what they were paying the person who left, but also to the market rate for the job. They did this and suddenly found that the right sort of candidates were applying for the position and they were fishing in a much bigger pool. It's a no-brainer.

The irony is, of course, that if they had kept a strategic eye on the market and paid their current staff market rate, they may not have lost him at all and would have saved themselves a lot of time and money. That's another story (look out for *The Book on Recruitment Part 2 – From Hired to Fired. What Goes Wrong with the Hiring Process in Other Businesses and How to Avoid It).*

So that leads us directly into the third point, which is deciding what you can afford. If you genuinely need all the skills and experience that you have put in your specification for the role, then you need to be prepared to either offer market rate or above, or offer something additional that the relevant candidates will accept as being very valuable and that will compensate for any gap in the salary. You may be able to offer to pay for training and certification. You may have a more than generous benefits system or an extremely good company pension plan. For some candidates this will compensate for any lack on the salary.

If you cannot afford to pay market rates for your wish list, then you must decide which parts of your wish list you can live without or outsource.

3. How to Create the Perfect Job Specification

You'll be happy to know that this is the easy part! And the even better news is this is the ONLY part of the process that most of your competitors will be doing and therefore you are already well ahead of them in your quest to become excellent at hiring great staff.

Start by thinking about exactly what you need the person to be able to do on a daily basis and jot it all down - make a list. Go through the day hour by hour what you foresee the person spending their time doing. As you go through the day, then the week and then the month thinking about all the differing tasks they will be doing, just jot them down – it doesn't matter if you have already put them on the list. Trust me. For now, just write them down.

The things that they will be spending the most time doing and/or the things that are most fundamental to the business are the essentials and will repeat themselves in your list. These things should come higher up the list on the job spec.

Lets work through that example. If you were looking to take on a customer services representative and felt that within two years you were going to need three of those and a customer services manager, then you would need to decide whether to take on an customer services representative now and hire a customer services manager later, or whether to hire someone who had the core competencies to progress to the next role. There are pluses and minuses to both routes. It would be simpler to hire "just a customer services representative," but that person might feel demotivated if you hired someone above them a couple of years down the line. If you decided to go for the progression route, then as well as the core daily duties of the customer services representative you would have to consider the core daily duties of the customer services manager.

You should also have a purpose for the role: what is the role there to achieve? If an employee knows what their part in the bigger picture is, then they are more likely to be able to achieve it.

So, in the case of a customer services adviser, the purpose of the role might be to make every customer's experience of dealing with the company a pleasurable one. It might be written as: to develop the relationship between our customers and our company and ensure that dealing with us is always easy and that we exceed customer expectations.

You can then go on to list the various parts of the role. In bullet point format they might be things like:

- To answer all telephone calls within five rings
- To resolve all customer issues within four hours
- Using the company's IT systems to find resolutions for customers queries
- To log all information on the database
- To call customers back at the agreed time
- To follow agreed scripts when dealing with existing new or lapsed customers

How much clearer and more powerful are the bullet points when they are preceded by the purpose of the role? Understanding the purpose of the role gives the employee the "why" behind all the bullet points.

The jobs spec should also contain any expectations of the role that may not be immediately obvious. For example, in the case of this customer services adviser who finishes work at 5 PM, you may expect them - if they are on a call at 5 PM for example - to continue with that call until it is finished rather than ending the call so they can end work at their official finish time. If that is the case, it should be specified, and also what compensation if any there will be for additional time worked – overtime pay or time off in lieu?

4. Creating the Perfect Person Specification

This can be a different document to the job spec (specification) or it can be part of the job spec, but it is actually the most crucial part of the recruitment process. To get this right will take some thought on your part.

I am sure you may have been in workplaces where there were people who just didn't fit in. They could do the job but they just weren't "our" kind of people. I guarantee you, those people have been hired purely on a job spec. The person spec is fundamental to the business, but most people don't even consider it. This is where interviewers use their "gut feeling."

So what's the problem with using gut feeling?

Well, there are a number of problems with it. Don't misunderstand me. I'm not saying you should never use gut feeling or you should ignore it. Far from it. Gut feeling is often right, but let's have a look at what it is and why it feels right.

Gut feeling, of course, is not some magic from outer space; it's not some skill that you can learn, or something that some people have and some people don't have. It's an accumulation of all your experience, of your ability to read people and of your empathy with others, and that's a combination of everything you've ever experienced in your entire life.

Some managers' gut feelings are very good – they are mostly "on the money," as they say. And that's great. However, even with these people, it's not always right, and even if it is, there are two problems with it.

The first problem is gut feeling is no defence in an employment tribunal. You can't say to the judge, "Well, I didn't take him on because I just had a bad feeling about him." That just won't wash. That will cost you thousands.

The second problem is this. Even if your gut feeling is right and you take someone on and that person is the best thing that ever happened your business, well, that is fantastic. However, as your business grows and you wish to get other people involved in the recruitment process or maybe even stop doing the recruitment yourself and leave it to your managers, let me ask you this: How do you teach somebody to have *your* gut feeling?

The answer is you can't. So you need to have a process by which you can deliver the same results as your gut feeling delivers but in an objective, logical, trackable and replicable manner. In this way, you have the benefit of being able to train yourself and your people to get consistent results and you cover yourself in the eyes of the law (at least in the UK).

The perfect person is the one that has the magic three ingredients. They have all the core competencies needed to be able to do the job properly. They have the attributes and values that will make them fit in. AND, they are motivated to do the job. More on that later.

The core competencies are those things without which the person hired will not be able to do that specific role, in that specific job, for that specific company – your company -- and on that specific team. If you have more than one team of people and more than one manager managing those teams, each of those teams is a micro culture and you will need to recruit accordingly if the managers and the team make-ups are different.

Let me explain that a little more.

I once worked for one of the U.K.'s largest employers. I was telesales person, then field sales representative, then senior sales/account manager, then telesales manager, field sales manager and then ran several teams and senior salespeople. As a senior manager, I had won various awards – including a team quality award (something normally won by an individual). A large part of the reason for those awards was that my team was stable with low staff turnover and great morale. It was for this reason that one of the senior managers in the business asked myself and a colleague to rewrite the internal recruitment procedures, since the staff turnover on my team was the lowest in the company at that time.

I didn't have a clue where to start because I didn't know what I was doing that was any different from anyone else. But I soon found out – HR were recruiting the same spec for each team. And managers were recruiting "mini me's."

You might think this is the logical thing for HR to do, and you would be right, but it is also the wrong thing. To be accurate, it is 33% the wrong thing. You can recruit against the job spec, but unless you are also testing for motivation and recruiting into the micro culture of the individual team, then it isn't going to work out.

For example, one of the managers I looked after was a micro-manager. They wanted to know the ins and outs of a small, feathered creature. The people who needed to be recruited to that team were those people – you know them – who want to be told the parameters of what they can do and prefer their manager to tell them what to do on a regular basis. In fact, if their manager doesn't tell them what to do (even though it is the same things as last week and the week before) they won't think about doing it themselves. They are too scared of getting it wrong and would much rather the manager take the flak if it all goes wrong. They can sit back and say, "Well, that's what I was told to do."

The other team needed grown ups. They had a manager who preferred to delegate total responsibility for the job to the individual. They had a "come and ask me if you need help, otherwise I will leave it to you" attitude. They needed a much more pro-active, responsibility taking, creative individual.

So, same job, same company, but two completely different types of individual required. Put either type of individual on the opposite team, and what do you create? Disharmony and unhappy staff leading to low motivation, poor results, and staff turnover.

So I put together a new competency-based framework for the company, which was based on how I recruited for my teams. This was based on the magic five – eight, which we will be talking about in Chapter 4.

So, where do you begin? In simple terms:

- Decide what you want
- Decide what you need
- Decide what you can afford
- Create the perfect job spec
- Create the perfect person spec

Logon to http://www.thebookonrecruitment.com and enter the unique code found at the end of this book to download a workbook on this chapter that includes a job and person specification template.

Now you have done the hardest bit: deciding what you want and need.

In Chapter 3, I am going to share with you the four most effective ways to find the people you want.

Chapter 3 - The Four Most Effective Ways to Find the People You Want

1. Recommendation

As someone who's been in recruitment since the mid-90s, you might not expect me to say that. However, why wouldn't you ask around? You don't know who in your circle of friends and work colleagues/clients/suppliers might know the perfect person for your business. It's easy. It's free. Why would you not do it? You absolutely should.

However – there's always a however isn't there? – there is one caveat.

Only take the cheapest option if it is also the best option.

I think this applies to everything in life and it absolutely, definitely, positively, applies to hiring staff.

In fact when hiring staff, it is the one rule you *must* always follow. If you get a free pen in an envelope through the door from a charity or from some business trying to sell you pens with an embossed pattern on it (I get those all the time) - then keep the pen. It's free. Use it. Why wouldn't you? Does it matter if only lasts for a day or a week? No it doesn't.

However, if you hire a member of staff through the free route, i.e. recommendation, and they don't work out, use up your time in training, make mistakes in your business that cost you money, disrupt your team, or God forbid somebody else leaves because of them or you lose clients because of their mistake....does that matter? It sure does.

Just because it's a recommendation, please do not circumvent the process. They *must* still fit the job spec and the person spec. You must identify the magic 5-8, and you must interview as you will learn to do in this book. Then, and only then, can you make an objective decision as to whether that person is the right person for your business. I cannot emphasise enough how important it is to not take the free option because it's free. It will cost you more in the long run.

Let's look at an example of that. A client of mine was looking for a manager to head up a completely new division of their business. Because this was a new role and one they had not recruited for before and one they were going to have to pay a considerable salary against, they decided to try and find somebody through recommendation and avoid advertising costs or an agency fee. So they asked around and they were introduced through a colleague to a lady who seemed to be perfect in every way. They liked and admired the person who recommended this lady and felt that supplier knew their business well enough to recommend someone appropriate.

Once the lady came to work for them, it fairly soon became apparent that her values and beliefs were not in line with theirs. Her customer service skills were negligible. She was a real hunter salesperson. She went after a lot of new business, but much of it she didn't win because of her abrasive manner. She also started having regular time off work with one or another complaint. The client decided they had made a mistake and scheduled a meeting with her to discuss her poor performance. She had been with them for approximately six months. On the day of the appointed meeting, a letter arrived from her solicitor saying that she was pregnant and the stress that they had been putting her under amounted to constructive dismissal and discrimination.

A very long process ensued which ended with the company having to pay this lady considerable amounts of money not to go to a tribunal. This was a commercial decision, mostly as they felt they did not want their managers or other staff involved in something as negative and draining as a tribunal process can be. They felt it better to pay off the lady in question and move on.

This happened because they allowed their assessment of the recommendation to interfere with the proper recruitment process which they would have used on any other candidate. So, I'll say it again, even if you're recommended someone who looks like a perfect candidate, please take off the rose-coloured spectacles and follow the proper process. If you don't, there is a very good chance you will regret it.

2. Advertising on or Off-line: The Old "Black Arts"

I could write a whole book on advertising; it is a massive subject. My flippant comment on advertising would be: if you're not an expert, don't waste your time and your money.

There are so many different places that you could advertise. There are local newspapers, national newspapers, magazines, online versions of all of the above, your website and various social media. You could do flyers to the local district (depending on the vacancy), you could put up posters or billboards, you could advertise in the local job centre, or you could go online to one of the many hundreds of job boards. Or you could do all of that, which of course would be extremely expensive.

How do you decide where to advertise? Well...you could look at what your competitors are doing, but that doesn't necessarily mean it's right place to advertise. If it's a local paper, you can bet your bottom dollar the salesperson will be ringing all of your competitors telling them they need to advertise in the publication because all of their competitors do. If a salesperson rings you with this line, ask for proof of results. Ask to speak to other companies in your field who have successfully filled similar vacancies using their paper. If they can't or won't provide these, then proceed with caution. Flies buzz round a honey jar, but they also buzz round a carcass!

We really don't have time to discuss the merits of each different form of online and offline media, but suffice it to say – consider your target audience and where they are likely to be looking.

Last week, I was having a conversation about one of the supermarkets (not any of the big boys) who were looking to recruit in Greater Manchester and had placed adverts only in Poland. When asked why, the reply was, "Well, we tried advertising in the local paper last time and got single-figure responses."

This was no surprise, since the local paper was not the main newspaper bought in the area, had a very small circulation and was not renowned for vacancy responses. The jobs on offer were 13 or 26-week contracts – ideal for jobseekers; the biggest proportion of job seekers in that area (in other words – those registered as out of work with the Job Centre) were 18 – 25 years old. Guess where most 18 – 25 year olds *don't* look for a job. Yep – you got it: the local newspaper.

For goodness' sake people; do a Facebook campaign, do something on YouTube which might generate a viral outcome, put your vacancy on the online job boards - even the Jobcentre has an online portal – but don't put it in the local paper if you are looking to attract that demographic.

As I said, consider your audience.

And if you don't know where your audience is looking, then don't waste your money trying different things – ask someone who knows. The local Chamber of Commerce should have business advisors to help you if you are a member. Ask around in networking groups where similar (but noncompeting) businesses advertise, or use an advertising agency who will not only know where to place your advert, but will also know what to put in the advert.

Or – if you can afford to – use an agency. There is no charge for registering your job with them. They will have access to a huge database of candidates and will know exactly where to find more – and all at no cost to you. It doesn't cost you to advertise, to look at CV's or to interview. It will only cost you *if* you hire someone. More about agencies later.

If you decide to do it yourself, how do you write a recruitment advert?

Most people get this bit very wrong.

They tell the job seeker what the job is and how great their company is.

But what's wrong with telling the job seeker what the job is, you say?

Well, the world has changed. It used to be the case that you could put an advert in the local paper saying that you needed a secretary who could type X number of words per minute to shorthand and work 9 to 5 Monday to Friday for a certain salary, and you would get lots of people applying for the job.

I will let you in on a secret. We are no longer in that world. Today's job seeker is picky.

They want to know why they should even bother applying for your job, not just what the job might entail. Despite everything you might hear about the jobs market - how many unemployed people there are, how many people looking for work (which may all be factually true) - ignore it, because it's not relevant.

The fact is that the profile of the average job seeker has changed over the past twenty years. Most people don't want to just do any old job. They want a job that in some ways reflects the work-life balance and the values and beliefs they hold. They want to work in a pleasant supportive environment. They want to be trained and developed. (One colleague of mine has this week started an eight-week temporary contract that has three weeks training first, before she starts! This company is obviously hoping to keep some of the temps afterwards.) They want to enjoy what they do. And they want a company and a product or service that they can believe in.

That may all sound very obvious to you and I, and actually it is.

However, most people when they write job adverts completely forget all of the above.

If you don't believe me, just pick up any local paper and have a look at the job adverts.

To illustrate the point, I just had a look online at the jobs advertised in our local paper, which is probably the most prominent paper in the greater Manchester area for job vacancies. Starting at a very basic level there were four adverts for gardeners. Two of them said, "Gardener required with full references." One advert said, "Semi-retired gardener sought for part-time work in the Worsley area." The last one said, "2 temporary gardeners required in the Miles Platting area, to do garden maintenance and cleaning. You may apply by e-mail or online at www.beourgardener.com (no that's not the website – don't apply for the job) and please note all applicants must fill in our application form, which we will email to you on request."

None of these adverts are very good, however, if I had to guess I would put money on the last two adverts generating more responses than the first two, because at least they mention the geographic area and give at least an indication of the hours and in one case how to apply.

Let's look at another example. In the same paper there were two adverts for cleaners. One of the adverts said, "Cleaner required, Wilmslow town centre, 5.30 till 7 PM Monday to Friday."

The second advert said, "Cleaner required £7.50 an hour." This is not the most exciting headline, but it went on to say 423 words about the employer, their mission, what they were looking for, the specific hours and the specific locations. It also said what was expected from the cleaners, what the main focus of the role was, what cleaning equipment they would be using and what types of rooms they would be cleaning. It also mentioned health and safety. The advert then said something about the type of person they were looking for in terms of character and experience. And it went on to discuss the training provided and the interview process.

This advert finished by stating how to apply, that the employer was an equal opportunities employer, and what the closing date for applications would be.

Alleluia! At last, a properly written advert.

Now, which of these two adverts do you think might generate the most response? Which would you be most interested in, if you are looking for a role as a cleaner? I think it's a safe bet to say that if you were a cleaner who was out of work and lived in the centre of Wilmslow, you would probably enquire about the Wilmslow role. However, you would also enquire about the other and plenty of people who didn't live in Wilmslow would be applying for the other role and not the Wilmslow one, even though they could probably commute there.

I have to tell you that this second advert was written by a recruitment agency, which isn't surprising because recruitment agencies know how to write adverts that will attract the right type of response and most direct employees don't.

The point that is illustrated here is that you need to think about what is attractive about your role and why someone should want to apply for it. It really doesn't matter whether it's a cleaner role, a low-level administration job or a crucial sales and marketing manager position. If you want the best possible person for that role, then you need to put a lot of thought into how you've written the advert, what you can offer the candidate, and more importantly, how you sell your opportunity to the potential employee.

For a free template on how to write an effective recruitment advertisements, go to http://www.thebookonrecruitment.com/templates and download one of the examples there.

3. Social Media: The New "Black Arts"

This is another massive subject and one I could devote a whole book to. Suffice it to say for now that more and more people are using social media to find a new job or their new employees.

Before you decide to use social media as a recruitment tool, and many companies – especially larger companies – do have an effective social media recruitment strategy, you must realise that once you have put your business into the limelight on social media, there's no going back. You can't just run the recruitment drive through social media; you need to have an entire social media strategy that puts out the right brand messages about your company and interacts with its followers.

The beauty of social media is that if you get it right, it's very cheap and you can reach many more people than with any other single medium. The danger is it's so easy to get it wrong and there's no point having a great recruitment drive planned through social media if your brand is either absent or not what it should be. You might as well not bother.

Most effective social media strategies involve building a bank of loyal followers to whom you can broadcast your messages and who will talk about you and your great company or great products and services or great job opportunities. It can also pay to advertise on Facebook, though this may not be as effective as having a bank of loyal followers to do your selling for you.

It used to be a case of "It's not what you know but who you know" to move up the career ladder or find the best opportunities, however, now millions of people are using social media to find their next opportunity. Which means that, as an employer, you need to consider using one or all of the available social media outlets to give you the broadest reach. There are tools such as http://www.Twitjobsearch.com where you can post your vacancies. At the time of writing you can also post vacancies to LinkedIn as long as you have an individual LinkedIn profile for around £130 per vacancy.

However, unless you already have a big network on LinkedIn, a big following on Twitter, or a business Facebook page with hundreds or thousands of people following you, using social media may not be the most effective way to find your next member of staff.

If you *do* want to use social media as part of your recruitment drive, I would suggest you use the facilities and knowledge of a digital marketing expert, otherwise you can spend an awful lot of time and money ineffectively.

4. The Last of the Four Methods (and arguably the most effective): Use a Recruitment Agency

As with the other three methods, this comes with a huge health warning.

Do not use a recruitment agency if any of the following statements are true:

- You do not have a well-defined job or person spec
- You can't be bothered or don't have the time to research and find a good agency who specialises in finding the type of candidates you are looking for
- You expect something for nothing
- You are not prepared to work with an agency, but just want CV's sending to you and don't think agencies deserve the fees they charge

If you didn't read the foreword and you don't know my background, I should probably tell you at this point that I have been involved in the world of recruitment since the early 90's, both in terms of recruiting internally for a large organisation, running a branch of a large IT recruitment consultancy for an international organisation, and also running my own recruitment consultancy since 2001.

I get it, I really do. I know that paying a recruitment agency is the last thing most companies want to do. It's a bit like paying your dentist. You know you need the work doing, you know you can't fix your own teeth but you really *really* resent having to pay for it. Because it's painful, because it sometimes goes wrong, because there are no guarantees you won't be back in the same position six months down the line, and possibly because you have either been dealing with the wrong dentist/agency and you don't really know what it is that they do for you.

So let's look at the reasons why you should use a *good* agency, and how to identify that.

There are six main reasons why you should use an agency and why it is preferable to any advertising you could do yourself.

1. Unless an agency finds you a suitable candidate for your vacancy and the candidate starts work at your company, then you owe the agency nothing. That can't be said of advertising or most other things in life. You have to pay your lawyer whether or not they win the case for you. You have to pay your accountant whether or not he saves you money, and you have to pay your architect even if you decide not to go ahead with the building work, because you are paying for their time

and their knowledge. You can't ring your local newspaper or a national newspaper and say, "Hey, I spent £1000 with you on recruitment advertising and I haven't been able to hire a suitable person. Can I have my thousand pounds back, please?" Well, you could say that, but the answer might not be printable!

So let me say it again, because it is a key point. Unless your agency finds you a suitable candidate who you believe is the perfect person for your job *and* you hire them *and* they start working for you, then you don't owe that agency a penny.

There is no risk to you.

The agency takes *all* the risk. They spend their time, their advertising resources, their staff wages, their telephone bills, their rent and rates, their stationery, their petrol and if they don't come up trumps and find you somebody suitable, then they have wasted a lot of time and money. But you don't owe them a penny.

2. The second reason why using an agency is more effective than advertising yourself is that the agency, if they specialise in finding the type of staff you are looking for, will already have a big bank of candidates with the skills that you need and a network of people and resources they can utilise to find other candidates with those skills. If you pick an agency that has been established any length of time, they will have literally

thousands of potential candidates on their database. That sort of choice would take you years to find.

3. The third reason why using an agency is better than advertising yourself is that, as a business owner, your time is invaluable. The more time you spend on non-core activities, the less money you make, and the reverse is also true. The more time you spend on your core activities and marketing your services, the more money you will make. To search through hundreds or thousands of candidates, reply to all advert responses, assess CV's, telephone screen potential suitable candidates, etc. takes an enormous amount of time. Whilst you are doing all that – who is running your business?

Typically, when we place an advert for a field sales person for a client, we can expect over 200 people to send their CV's. Do you have time to effectively deal with 200 CV's? Possibly...if you're prepared to take a month or so to fit in round your normal activity. However, the problem with that is that after a month, most of those people will have found other jobs, and you will have wasted a lot of your time. And if you don't respond to them at all – well, that's your reputation as a company tarnished. So it's imperative once you start a recruitment drive to act quickly. The best candidates will have other job opportunities. They will have other interviews lined up. If you don't get back to them within twenty-four hours of them applying for your role then you can kiss them goodbye in most cases.

Ask yourself, "Do I have the time to take a week or two weeks out of my business to devote entirely to the recruitment process?" Most business owners really don't.

If you use an agency, they will do the finding and the screening of the candidates for you. You can then have a look at a small amount of CV's, or if you work with the right agency and trust them to screen properly, you can go straight to first interview without even having to make spend any time on CV assessment.

Okay, so if you've decided not to use an agency, move to the next chapter now. However, if you think it might be an option for you now or in the future and you have the financial resources to do so, then how do you choose a good one?

There are some obvious things that you should do. The first one is to ask for a referral. If you have friends who are also in business or who are employees but hire staff, ask them who they use. Remember, though, if they are potentially competitors (I don't just mean in the same business as you, but potential competitors for the talent in the market place) then they may not want to tell you.

Get a list of agencies together - either from referral or just by using Google. For example, "recruitment agencies Salford construction" (which brought back 350,000 results just now!). Once you've done that there are a few things you should do.

Firstly, look at their website. Is it up-to-date and does it tell you about themselves, or about what they will do for you? If it is outdated (no Blog, no Twitter or other social media feeds, no Facebook page, no LinkedIn presence for the company/staff), consider what that says about their use of technology - especially since most candidates nowadays are generated through technology/social media - and be wary. Look how long they've been established. If they've been in business more than ten years then that says something about how good they are. Recruitment is a tough old world and those agencies that can survive and have longevity must be doing something right. Of course, younger agencies can also be good and may be around themselves in ten years time, so it's not everything.

Look at whether they are members of the REC (in the UK – the Recruitment and Employment Confederation) and whether their staff are REC trained. If they are REC members as a company, that's great. But you can buy REC membership as you can buy membership to a number of organisations such as the Federation of Master Builders or the Chamber of Commerce.

If you bought REC membership, it means you want to have the logo, which means you care what people think, but it doesn't necessarily mean that you're any good. No one from REC comes to visit your agency, and no one from REC asks to speak to any of your clients or candidates. They do look at your terms and conditions and make sure they're legally compliant, which is great.

And they take a couple of supplier references. But basically having REC membership just means you care about your business enough to have the logo.

On the other hand, if the people within the agency are REC qualified, then that means something. To be REC qualified you have to do a home study course or distance learning course. You have to do four modules which cover the law, the marketplace, clients and candidates. And then you have to take an exam – and pass it. So if you have the REC qualifications after your name, then you have some idea of what you are talking about. My advice is, when you speak to an agency, check if their staff have the REC qualification and if they don't, move on.

Don't neglect to check out the owners of the recruitment business on LinkedIn. If they're not on LinkedIn, perhaps you should question how extensive their networks are and how important they rate social media. If they have a profile, have a look at how many testimonials they have, what those testimonials say and who those testimonials are from. If they are all reciprocal (i.e. from people who they themselves have given testimonials to) or ex colleagues, then take them with a pinch of salt.

So there are things you can do to identify an agency you may wish to work with. You may want to look at their Facebook page if they have one as you may want to be involved with a business that cares about and is involved in the local community. You may want to deal with an agency that is extremely niche in the type of candidates that they can procure.

Once you contact one or more agencies, see if they offer to visit you. If they don't, then be careful about proceeding. In order for an agency to correctly identify the right candidates for a business, they must understand the culture and values of that business and they must be able to sell that business to their candidates. If they haven't seen your premises and if they haven't met your team and if they haven't soaked in the atmosphere of your business, how can they identify the right candidates or sell your opportunity to them?

Once you have decided on an agency that you wish to work with, please don’t tie their hands behind their backs. Allow them to do their job properly and give them the information and the time that they need to do the best possible job for you. The agency will tell you how they need to work with you in order to be as effective for you as they can. As far as humanly possible, work with them in the way they need to work because by doing that you will get the result you want. The important thing is communication and speed of communication. So make sure you take the time to fully explain your company culture, your vision, your plans and the job and person spec to the agency including all the selling points of your business. In that way, the agency can do (nearly) as good a job as you would do in selling your company and answering the candidates' questions about the role. And please make sure you are speedy in your response to CVs, queries, to interview requests, second interview requests and making an offer. Many a great candidate has been lost through procrastination on the part of the business.

Running a small business myself, I fully appreciate that sometimes other priorities come up. However, once you have decided to partake in a recruitment drive, that must be your priority. If it isn't, you will waste both your own and your agency's time. And as we discussed earlier, an agency gets no money unless they fill your vacancy and that person starts work. If you waste their time you are costing them money and costing yourself money. However, if you work with them you can form a lasting relationship with a company who will get to know your business inside out and will save you an invaluable amount of time over the years.

There are other methods of finding candidates, but the four we've discussed in this chapter are the four most effective methods. Whichever you choose, the next chapter is the most important and the heart of the entire recruitment process. If you get this bit right you will be able to identify and therefore hire the right people for your business.

So are you ready for the exciting bit?

Chapter 4 - The Magic of 5 – 8

As I've indicated earlier in the book, most people start the recruitment process at entirely the wrong place.

They start with the job spec. Whilst this is understandable, it is entirely the wrong place to start. What you should start with is a total understanding of what your company is. What do you stand for? What is your brand? What matters to you? And also, where are you heading? What are the longer term plans? Once you have identified these factors then you can look at the job that you need filling and the personal qualities of the ideal candidate for the job.

The job skills are the easy part to identify. If someone needs to have previous experience of your industry, if they need certain qualifications or technical skills, if they need another language, if they need a level of physical fitness - for example to be a firefighter - all those things are the easy things to identify.

The magic of recruitment is in identifying the 5 to 8 competencies that are fundamental to a long-term successful hire for that role in your company.

These 5 to 8 competencies, as we call them, are normally the things that can't be trained. They are qualities such as drive, resilience, positive mental attitude, sense of humour, attention to detail, team player, independence, responsibility, creativity, or honesty, for example. These are the things without which the person will be unsuccessful in that job.

It has been my experience that there are three important factors in recruiting for a job. Firstly, can the person do the job? This means do they have the skills? Technically and by experience, do they fit the job spec? The second and third - i.e. 66% of what is important is about the person, in almost equal parts - are they motivated to do the job, and are they a culture fit?

Somebody may be technically able to do the job that you have on offer but for whatever reason may not be motivated to do it. Maybe they don't want to be a software developer anymore. Maybe they want to be a team manager or maybe they want to go start the gardening business that has always been their dream but haven't got the means or knowledge to do that.

Or even if they are motivated to do your job, will they fit in? If they are very into technology and are very up-to-date with modern methods of communication and marketing, will they fit into a very traditional office where e-mail is still used in preference to text or Instant Messenger or Facebook or any of the other emerging technologies? If they are quite serious and shy, will they fit into an office full of gregarious laughter-makers?

To reiterate - because it is vitally important that I get this bit across to you - 66% of hiring the right person has nothing to do with the job spec. So how do you identify that 66%?

The best way to do this is with a brainstorming session. If there is only you in the business, think about the qualities and values that you have and that you believe your business stands for. What are the qualities that you need to see in your first employee in order to for you to be able to work with them. Do you need somebody like you? Or do you need somebody to balance you? If you are the salesperson in your business, do you need another you, or do you need somebody who is a "finisher" (technical speak for someone who will actually get things done that you have started).

If your business is slightly bigger, what is the culture of the team? What dynamics are going on within the team? What additional competencies would you like to bring to the team? Or are you looking for a replica of the people you already have?

I don't think I can over emphasise how important this stage of the process is.

Actually, it's a pretty important part of running a business in general. This is something a lot of small businesses either don't do at all, or they did it once and then forgot about it in the busy-ness of running the daily operation. The reality is that this understanding of who you are as a business, what your brand represents, and how you want to interact with your prospective market is fundamental to everything you do in the business and not just in the recruitment of staff. It runs through how you will market your business, your corporate social responsibility activities, your corporate development, which products and services you offer, and how you offer them. In short, it is the foundation for everything.

It is so worthwhile to take the time to put pen to paper and identify this vision of your company values and what your brand looks and feels like and stands for. For more help with this, go to http://www.thebookonrecruitment.com and look for the exercise on identifying company values.

Once you have a clearer understanding of your company vision, you can then look at your short, medium and long term plans. In recruitment terms, this is important to do because the skills and attributes you're looking for in an employee to have right now may need to change over time and therefore, if you can recruit with an eye to the future, is likely to be more effective and longer term.

Okay, so you are now ready to draw up your job and person spec.

The job spec as discussed is the easy bit that involves drawing up a thorough job description, including all the activities this person will have to be involved in. You will easily be able to create a job spec that identifies the skills required. When looking at the person spec ,the question underlying everything is, "Will the person fit in here?" In order to be sure that they will "fit in here," you need to be looking for the attributes that match the company's vision and values, which is the purpose of doing the previous exercise.

If you know what the company's values are, what the brand is, and how you want to interact with your customers, then you can easily identify the personal qualities that will fit with those values.

To make it easier, think of it this way. Generally, things that are trainable or knowledge that is acquired through experience are usually the things that will go on the job spec. Those things that are not trainable will generally go on the person spec.

What you are looking for ideally is between five and eight competencies, without which that person will not be able to do that specific role, in that specific team (if you have more than one team), in your company.

They may be able to do a similar role technically in another company, but the technical skills, as we discussed, are the easy bit.

The competencies are what will give you some confidence that you are identifying a good match to your company culture and values. For example, let's imagine you run a sales company or a sales team. One of the ways that you differentiate your company from others in your field is in the level of customer service that you give. Your interactions with your customers leave them feeling nurtured and looked after rather than sold to. One of the ways that you achieve this is by being quietly persistent. You have a good follow-up system and marketing activity is targeted to keep in touch with people without blatantly selling to them, because you know that on average it takes nine contacts from you for your customers to buy.

Given the above scenario, two of the qualities that you will probably need in your next salesperson are resilience and empathy. There's no point in having a company culture of customer service and nurturing your customers, backed up by a fantastic marketing initiative that uses automatic IT systems to keep in touch with potential clients, if you then employ a hard-core, knock-the-door-down salesperson who is like a terrier going after the sale.

That person could do more damage to the reputation of your company and your brand then you might imagine. And although they might be a great salesperson and able to get orders, they are not going to fit with your culture. Which means that they are not going to be happy in your culture because they won't be recognised for the work they do. They are more likely to be criticised, as their style will probably upset your customer base and possibly the rest of the team. So you can see how important it is to make sure that the competencies you are looking for when you're interviewing match the cultural values of the company and of the team or the company as a whole.

The other benefits of doing this work is that it then spills over into the whole life of that individual as an employee of your company. You will use the same competencies when doing appraisals, when looking at personal development plans, when looking at sales targets or KPI's (key performance indicators), so whilst this may seem like a lot of work to do on day one and for one hire, in the long run this will save you lots of time and make your whole business more "joined up."

Getting hiring matters right is not a separate issue to be dealt with once in a blue moon, or whenever hiring; it is fundamental to the entire business – or it should be!

So spend a few minutes now if you are currently recruiting, or even if you're not, to do the exercise on company culture and values. Once you've done that, look at the next role you are likely to recruit and decide what the 5 to 8 key competencies for that role will be. You may find that in many cases the key competencies for most roles will be similar. There may be two or three that differ for each role depending on the type of role - whether it's a management role, technical role or a creative role - but some of the competencies will be the same in every role because they reflect the values and brand of the company.

One way to test whether something is a core competency or not is to imagine this. During the interview you were unable to discover any evidence of one of the competencies. If the candidate had good evidence of all the other competencies would you still be happy to recruit them? If the answer is yes, then that probably is not a core competency but a "nice to have," because as we said at the beginning, core competencies are the ones without which someone will not be able to do the role successfully long-term.

For a full list of potential competencies go to http://www.thebookonrecruitment.com and download the competencies checklist.

Chapter 5 - Questioning for Competency

You will be happy to know there is a method to doing this. We call it behavioural interviewing, and there are three parts to it. The first is to identify the competency that you are looking for. The second is deciding what behaviours you would see in someone who had that competency. The third part is framing questions around those behaviours that will get you the information that you need in order to make an objective decision.

We did part one in the last chapter, and part two is identifying the behaviours that you would see in someone with that competency in your particular role.

Let's look at how to do that and go back to the competency of resilience that we mentioned previously. If you are recruiting for a salesperson and one of the competencies you were looking for was resilience, what behaviours would you expect to see in a successful salesperson that would show you that they were resilient?

Would it be things like...the person comes off an unsuccessful call and immediately makes the next call?

Would it be that the person is self-analytical? Do they look at why they missed last month's target/last week's target, identify the reasons and then put in place actions that will ensure that this week's or this month's target is achieved?

Is it that they have a positive attitude at all times? Perhaps it is that they are realistic about their own achievements and have high self-esteem?

This last one is quite important. Many salespeople have low self-esteem and the reason they're in sales is because they need the constant reinforcement of achieving daily or weekly targets to prove to themselves that they are good, that they are worth something.

The problem with salespeople who have low self-esteem is that they often lack resilience. Self-esteem is often what gets you through the bad patches, and in sales, every day is not going to be brilliant, every single week is not going to be brilliant. Sometimes, depending on the life cycle of the sale, not every quarter or financial year is going to be brilliant. You will find that the salesperson who has self-esteem, who knows that not everything is their fault but takes responsibility for their results rather than looking for someone or something to blame - they have long-term resilience. And it is this quality which will save them from the many "no's" and the many disappointments that a career in sales can bring.

Once you have identified a behaviour (and you need two to three behaviours for each competency), you can then frame your questions.

In order to be an effective question, it must relate to the behaviour and it must be in the past tense so that you are talking about reality. The best indicator of future performance is past performance. Therefore, you need to ask questions about the person's real life experiences in order to understand how they are likely to exhibit those behaviours or competencies in the future.

So a behavioural question around the competency of resilience could be "Tell me about the last time that you had a run of customers not buying from you and what you did about it." It's important that you dig into enough detail in the answers (if the candidate does not volunteer enough detail), and you can use a technique called SOARE to ensure that you have the detail you need.

S.O.A.R.E. stands for Situation, Objective, Action, Results, and Emotion. And you would use it in the following manner:

You: "So tell me about the last time you had a string of customers who all said no to you, perhaps in a situation where it looked like you might then miss your target for the month." (Situation)

The candidate replies: "Yes, I recently had a week where the first four customers I went to see all said no."

You ask, "Okay that sounds tough. So what was your reaction in that situation?" (Objective)

Candidate replies, "My plan was to make sure I got at least two sales out of the next two days."

"Okay," you reply, "so how did you plan to do that?" (Action)

The candidate replies, "I phoned around and put an extra three appointments in my diary, making a total of six appointments in the next two days."

You ask, "So what happened?" (Results)

The candidate replies, "Well, actually I had a rather good run and a 50% conversion rate, so I actually made three sales, but two of them were from the extra three appointments and if I hadn't put those in, I would have missed my target."

You reply, "Well done. So how did that make you feel?" (Emotion)

Candidate replies, "I felt really good because I knew the appointments had directly impacted me getting the result that I wanted, in fact, a better result than I needed. I gained the confidence that if that situation happened again, I would be able to find a way to hit target."

In that particular scenario you may want to dig further and ask why they thought their conversion rate was better than normal, what type of customers they were talking to, where they got their extra appointments from or other questions. The more detail you can get within the answers, the more likely it is that the candidate is telling you the truth.

And this is the key to why all behavioural questions should be grounded in the past.

It is much more difficult for a person to lie in specific detail than it is for them to make broad generalisations or describe something without specific detail or talk about the theoretical – what they would do in a given situation. Behavioural questions must be centred in the past. The best indicator of future performance is past performance.

There is really only one exception to this rule.

If one of the competencies you are looking for is the ability to think on your feet or to be spontaneously creative, you may want to ask theoretical questions - just to see how that person's brain works and how quickly they can come up with a new idea. But this would be planned. You should not use theoretical questions to test most competencies, as they do not tell you what a person has done or would do, in that scenario, only what they *think* they would do – or more probably – what they think you want to hear them say they would do. Past behaviour is the best indicator of future behaviour, and yes, I know I have said that three times now. It was intentional!

This is a really simple concept, but one that most people get wrong.

In an interview most business owners/hiring managers would ask the following questions or ones like them:

How would you handle an angry customer?

What would you do if your boss came to you with extra work that you knew you wouldn't be able to complete?

What would you do if the team were close to missing a sales target?

If the project you were working on looked like it was going to miss the deadline, what would you do about that?

These all *look like* valid questions on the surface, but none of them are behavioural.

Think about how to turn those questions into behavioural questions. For the answers to this plus a list of behaviours and questions that you can ask around those behaviours, go to www.thebookonrecruitment.com and download the behaviours check list and some sample behavioural interviewing questions.

Chapter 6 - The Proven 10-Step Process to Planning a Successful Interview

Step one: Read the CV

Study the CV so you know the background of the person you are about interview. This sounds really obvious, but so many interviews start with, "Why don't you begin by talking me through your CV?". This is lazy interviewing and generally means the interviewer has not bothered to spend the time to read the CV.

There are many things you can pick up from the CV, such as icebreaker questions. These are questions that you would ask right at the beginning of the interview to put the interviewee at their ease. A good place to look for clues as to icebreaker questions is in the hobby section or perhaps the school/college or university the person attended, a gap year they took, or any voluntary work they are involved with.

You can then ask something such as, "I see that you do Tae Kwon Do in your spare time. How often do you go to class? I always fancied doing that martial art - would you recommend it?". This sort of question can do exactly what it says on the tin – it can break the ice and start to build rapport between you and the candidate. It will also give you an idea of their true personality. When someone is talking about their hobby or something that interests them outside of work, their defences naturally drop slightly, they can become more animated and you'll get a better feeling for the real person.

Other things to look for in the CV are spelling, punctuation and grammar. If this is poor, you can draw your own conclusions. It's entirely a matter of opinion, however, if someone is coming for a job and they have not taken the time to check their CV, or to get someone else to check it, then that tells you something about the person. Be careful though, because people with dyslexia, for example, even if they use a spellchecker, may still have difficulty producing a piece of written work with no errors.

Something else to look for is obvious gaps in the CV. Always question gaps. If you are using an agency ask them, but ask again in the interview to make sure the two answers match. There are some very legitimate reasons for gaps. It could simply be that they were looking for a job. Or perhaps there was a perfectly reasonable family matter – a death in the family or a serious illness. Perhaps they were taking a bit of time off for a personal project – building an extension, or even writing a book. But there are other reasons that need to be investigated. It could be that the person was ill, or in prison. Neither of these things would necessarily make them unsuitable for your position, however, you may want to be aware of them.

In any case, reading the CV will put you in the right frame of mind and provide the focus you need to start preparing for the interview.

Step Two: Social media. To Use or Not to Use?

Proceed with caution with the use of social media and recruitment – see David Walton's comments by going to www.thebookonrecriutment.com and downloading "The Legals". However, what is in the social domain is in the social domain. People would fully expect you to check their LinkedIn profile (if they have one) when applying for a job, and indeed you should always do that. You will get a useful insight into whether they have any testimonials, how they have presented themselves, and whether they are good networkers. You may also feel you want to search for them on Facebook or Google.

As I say, Facebook and Google are both in the public domain and therefore anybody can access them at any time. My advice would be if you're going to use these tools, use them for every person you interview so that you cannot be accused of discriminating and only, for example, using social media to look at the profile of your potential female employees or of ethnic groups.

If social media is going to be part of your recruitment process, and I personally suggest that it is, make sure it is a process - a structured process - that you use for every applicant. Also, don't use it as a defining factor. The current generation uses Facebook as the baby boomers would've used the telephone - to chat incessantly to all their friends, all night long. The difference now is conversations are on a more public basis than they would have been then, and once they're out there in the public domain you can’t really take them back. So use social media sensibly and appreciate that whilst some people are comfortable having part of their life on display, and you may not be comfortable with, it doesn't mean they can't do the job. It just means they might need to grow up a bit.

Step Three: Setting up the Interview Room

The interview room should, if possible, be quiet, private and comfortable. I would not normally recommend interviewing someone in an open office where other people can overhear, unless one of the competencies you are looking for in your interviewee is the ability to work under extreme pressure.

I've seen many interviewers play "bad cop." This is very 1980s and without doubt not the best way to get to know your potential new employee. More about this in Chapter 7.

On this basis, and in terms of room setup, I suggest that you do not sit on the opposite side of the desk from your applicant. This puts an immediate barrier between you and it says to the interviewee, “I hold the power and you don't.”

The absolute best way to make an objective selection of candidates is to get to see as much of the real them as you possibly can. The only way to do that is to build rapport, make them feel comfortable so that they feel they can tell you anything. Even things they probably shouldn't tell you in an interview.

Therefore, if you have a desk or a coffee table, make sure you are sitting on the same side, or on two adjoining sides. Make sure the candidate’s seat is comfortable, at the same height as your seat (because if your seat is higher, we are back to the "I hold the power" scenario) and not facing the window. The afternoon sun streaming in directly into their eyes will do wonders to put them off! Amazing and possibly amusing as it seems, this is interview advice that you would have found twenty years ago in some sources.

The advice then would have been to put the candidate in an awkward position to “see how they cope." This is what buyers have been trained to do to salespeople. It's not what you should be doing in an interview with a prospective employee.

Make sure the room is at an ambient temperature, not too hot, nor too cold. If someone is thinking about how hot or cold they are, they are not going to give a hundred per cent focus to the interview, and neither are you.

I once had a director of a company, where I was a senior manager, interview a candidate I had already interviewed and really liked. When he came out of the interview he said, "I wouldn't take her on." His reason for this was that she had taken her jacket off during the interview. He interpreted this as an attempt to influence his decision. I interpreted it as the results of the room being 30°. I took her on. She became one of my top consultants, and after several years she left and started her own business, which she subsequently successfully sold.

So be careful how you interpret things that happen in an interview, and if possible, make sure that there are no negative influencing factors in the environment. Which brings me to step four.

Step Four: Interruptions

This is quick and easy. Recruiting a member of staff is possibly and arguably the most important thing that you can do to grow your business. It deserves your full attention. Do not allow interruptions. Turn your phone off, and if you want to make sure the candidate has turned their phone off, then make a point of turning off your phone at the beginning of the interview saying, “Oh, I had better make sure my phone is switched off; is yours?” If you have any other staff, make sure they know they are to take messages and phone calls and not interrupt you unless the building is burning down.

Apart from the fact that it is vital for you to focus on the interview and ensure you have a successful outcome (whatever that may be), it is also important that the interviewee is given the best chance. If there are interruptions, this will disrupt their thought process and might add to the stress they may already be feeling. That's not fair to them and it's not fair to you and it won't help you make a decision.

End of the lecture.

Step Five: Competency Questions

Make sure you have your list of competencies, behaviours and behavioural questions that you have determined before the interview. Ask all of these questions to each interviewee and note down their answers. Making notes is very important. Unless you have a photographic memory, after you have conducted a couple of interviews or after a time has elapsed - which could be five minutes, five hours, or five days, depending on the individual - you will have forgotten some of the things that the interviewee said. In order to make a proper assessment between candidates you must have comprehensive notes to refer to.

If you are not able to conduct the interview and ask questions and take the notes in a reasonably fluid manner then consider having someone else in the room who can take the notes, or use a tape recorder - though if you do the latter, you should point it out to the candidates and ensure they have no objections to that. In any case my advice would be to get someone else in to take the notes. If it's someone within your company or a colleague whose opinion you value, they may be able to shed some interesting light and give their opinion on anything you're not clear about.

There is some debate as to where competency questions should come within an interview. There are two schools of thought on this.

You can inform the candidate you are looking for certain competencies and therefore will be asking questions around those competencies. You would then go straight into those questions first, and then ask any factual questions after (see step six). Or you can reverse that and do the factual questioning first and competences second. It doesn't matter hugely; factual questions tend to be "easier" to answer in that the candidate is probably expecting them and therefore has prepared answers for them. Asking factual questions first can get the conversation flowing.

Equally, it can be good to get the more difficult, competency-based questions done first and then the candidate can breathe a sigh of relief in the latter stages of the interview when they have the "easier" questions to answer.

Step Six: Factual Questions

Whilst the competency questions should be the same for each candidate for a specific role so that you can fairly assess the answers against each other, the factual questions will of necessity be different.

These questions will include the icebreakers, technical (skills-based) questions, the questioning around any gaps on the CV, reasons for leaving previous roles, targets and achievements (in the case of sales people) and qualifications (see below). It may incorporate technical tests – writing a piece of code, typing tests, maths tests, etc. – depending on the role.

You may want to pick up on any project accomplishment or achievement mentioned in the CV or that has been brought up during the competency questions. If relevant to you, you may wish to ask about the qualifications someone has, and then you may wish to ask a few questions which would apply to all applicants, such as where do you want your career to go? Where would you like to be in five years' time? What would be the most interesting part of this role for you? Why did you apply for this role in the first place? Why should we give you the job? If you are going to ask these questions, make sure you ask all applicants in the interests of fairness and to help you properly assess.

With factual questions, always think, "What is the purpose of asking this question?" Don't ask questions just to fill time. The only exception to this rule is the icebreaker questions, but there is still a purpose to those, which is to put the candidate their ease.

Some factual questions that you may wish to include would be around any 'must-have' qualifications or technical knowledge, around dates, length of experience (and ensure this is actually required for the role and not a case of age discrimination), the motivation for leaving their current employment if they are in employment, their notice period, whether they drive and have their own car (if required for the role), why they applied for your role and whether they have any questions for you.

Step Seven: The Beginning, the Middle and the End

There is an old adage in sales: "Tell them what you are going to tell them...then tell them...then tell them what you have told them." This applies to an interview process quite well.

At the beginning, tell them what is going to happen – the structure of the interview and when they can ask their questions. So you might say something like this:

"Hello, Jack/Mr Smith, nice to meet you. My name is Carole and I am the Managing Director. As you are aware, I am looking for a personal assistant so what I would like to do today is this: I have identified exactly what competencies are going to be required to make someone successful in this role, so I'm going to be going through a series of questions that relate to that. We will also talk about your background, what your career plans are and why you are interested in this role. At the end of this there will be time for you to ask any questions you may have and I'll explain to you what will be happening next. Is that okay?"

The next icebreaker might go like this: "So, Jack, I see that you like reading biographies in your spare time. What's the most recent biography you've read?"

The middle of the interview is just about asking the competency-based and factual questions that you decided on beforehand and recording or getting somebody else to record the answers.

At the end of the interview, you will ask for their questions and then (in this order) talk to them about the job, the company and the future as you see it. And you will close them. I will explain what I mean by that.

We are going to look at each of the steps in more depth below in steps 8 (their questions), 9 (sell the company and the future) and 10 (close them), but after you have done that you will then tell them what will be happening next. If you're seeing other candidates, tell them when, so that you can give them an idea of when they will hear back from you. That might be to invite them back for another meeting, whether that be for a second interview or to meet the team or to undertake some kind of testing, or regarding letting them know whether they have been successful for the job or not.

It is very important to remember that you are not the only opportunity on the market. So whilst it is important not to rush the process and make bad decision, it *is* important to be a speedy as possible. If candidates have other interviews going on (and you will know this if you follow step 10) then it is absolutely vital that you act in a speedy manner. There is nothing worse than spending a long time deliberating and finally coming to a decision to offer a perfect candidate the job only to find that the day before they accepted a job somewhere else. Even if you are their preferred job, in this market a bird in the hand is worth two in the bush, as the old expression goes.

If you are working with an agency they will push you to make a decision quickly. They are not doing this for their benefit, but for yours. Well, I will qualify that somewhat; it is also for their benefit. Most agencies in the UK work for free until your new member of staff starts working for you. Let's say they've spent a week of their time interviewing candidates and arranging interviews for you and then you don't move fast enough and the candidate you finally decide that you want has taken a job through another agency. Your agency then has to start all over again and do another week's work for free! You can see how this would not enhance your working relationship. In recruitment terms, timeliness is important – so don't procrastinate!

Step Eight: Their Questions

Make sure you leave time towards the end of the interview for their questions. If this is their first interview with you, they should have some questions. What you really want to hear at this point is intelligent questions such as "Where do you see the company going?" "What are the growth plans?" "Where could I be in five years time?" "What do you think makes you stand out from your competitors?" "Why did you start the business?"

You want to hear anything that shows that they're genuinely interested in you, your job and your company. What you don't really want to hear at this point is "What are the holidays?" "Do I get paid overtime?" "What are the pension arrangements/ healthcare /benefits?"

It's not that people won't want to know those things or that they shouldn't want to know those things. But what you really want is somebody who wants the *job*, not somebody who wants the salary and benefits package.

Be as honest as you can, without breaching any confidentiality, in your answers to their questions. Don't "big it up" and make it sound better than it is, but equally, don't dumb it down or make the job sound easier. If you do either of these things and the person takes the job on the basis of what you've told them, then expect them to leave within three to six months when they have realised the job and the prospects are not as explained to them in the interview.

Step Nine: Sell the job, the Company and the Future

It is very important that you do this. And it is very important that you do this NOW - at the end of the interview. Most interviewers don't do this step at all. That's just plain daft. You are not the only option in the marketplace. You are (probably) not yet a household name, with people clamouring to join your company, as they do with Google or Facebook. Therefore, you need to paint a picture of why this person should want to come and work for you.

If you're working with an agency, you will be able to ask the agency what motivates the candidate and target your response to that. That doesn't mean making anything up, but it does mean that if job security is very important to this person but healthcare is not, then you should spend the majority of your time discussing how secure the job is.

If you are not working with an agency, then you should have picked up from the candidate's questions what is important to them. Make sure that during the time you are selling the job and the company to them, you are addressing those priorities. There is no point talking about stuff that is of no interest. At my previous company, one of the benefits was dental care. That was of no interest to me as I already have dental care as part of the general health plan that I have.

Much more important to me was the company car scheme. I had a company car with my previous company and didn't want to get my own - although if I was taking the job today I would definitely not want a company car because of the very unfavourable tax implications of company cars in the UK in 2012.

The other important reason for selling the job, company and the future at the end of the interview is quite obviously if you do that at the beginning of the interview then the candidate knows exactly what you are looking for and will tailor their responses in the light of that. This is not very useful in helping you make an objective decision and therefore should be avoided.

Step Ten: Close Them

This is something - I can promise you - that almost never happens in an interview. I think it comes from the old-school, and possibly quite British, belief that when you are interviewing *you* are the one with something to offer. The candidate should be grateful to get a job offer from anyone. Or maybe it's just because people don't like to be pushy and closing is a "sales thing."

If you don't close someone at the end of an interview, you have missed a massive opportunity. In my experience of being interviewed, only one company closed me by the end of an interview and that was the IT recruiter I subsequently worked for.

Honestly, it's not as scary as it sounds.

It's the ideal time to do it because you have just sold the job, the company and the future to this candidate, and you have targeted that to the information that is most important to them. They should be feeling quite good about the opportunity at this point.

This is your ideal chance to ask them whether they have other interviews that they are waiting to hear back from and if they do, how do they feel about yours in relation to that? You should ask if there is anything they are unsure about that they wish to clarify? And if not, and they don't have other interviews going on, then you can ask them something like, "If we were to ring you tomorrow and offer you the job, would you accept?"

If they say, “Well, I would have to think about it,” then that is your opportunity to ask what it is they would like to think about. If they need to think about it, then there is something that they either have not told you or that they are not clear about. If it's the former, you may feel uncomfortable about pushing for information. If it's the latter, this is your opportunity to clear up any grey areas.

They may say, for example, “Well, it's a big step up for me and I feel I would need some training in the area of X.” Don't immediately answer whatever they say first, because it is a bit like when you go to the doctor and they ask what's wrong. The first thing they say to you may not be the real problem.

The best thing to do is to clarify what they just said and then ask - and this is very important - ask exactly these words: "And what else?" And then shut up. The silence may be uncomfortable, but let them fill it. If there's nothing else, they will say, “No - that's my only problem.” However, it is likely that they may say, “Well actually, I was a bit worried about Y.” In this way, you get to the real crux of the issue and have the opportunity to cover it and solve it.

You can then close them (yes, there’s that scary word again) by saying something like, “Okay, so you are happy that X is not a problem, and we've talked about what we can do about Y. Now, I do have other people to see tomorrow, so I will be making a decision on Friday. If the decision is to offer you the job, would you accept it?” If they then say yes and you feel it is appropriate, you can then ask at what salary they would accept. If you are working with an agency that should have already been covered.

If they won't commit at this stage, then you really need to think hard about whether they are the person you want to offer the job to. If they can't commit at interview stage, when they should be at their most enthusiastic, they either don't really want the job or there is something else they are not telling you about. In which case you need to think about whether you want an employee who keeps important stuff from you. Just a thought.

Chapter 7 - Can I Ask You a Question? The Tried and Tested Do's and Don'ts of Effective Questioning

1. Be Polite

As discussed in the previous chapter, there really is no reason or justification for being rude and aggressive or overly confrontational in an interview. The reason for this should be fairly obvious, but let's look at a real-life scenario.

Once upon a time, in a kingdom not too far from here, I was interviewed by this style of interviewer. He was *very* confrontational during the interview, and patronising. I defended my corner in the interview, which was obviously the "right" thing to do in this man's eyes, as he put me forward for a second interview. I almost didn't go to the second interview because I thought to myself, "If that is the kind of person who works in this company, I am not sure I want to work there." The only reason I went for the second interview was that a colleague of mine was married to someone who worked in that company and they persuaded me that this man was a one-off. Apparently, he was known for being like a sergeant major (indeed, he had been one in a previous life in the Queen's Guards).

So I reluctantly went to the second interview. I got the job and I worked for that company for ten years, was highly successful, and made them a lot of money. And all of that nearly didn't happen because of one untrained interviewer. And that was a shame really, because once I worked there for a while and got to know this person properly, he was really nice. He passionately cared about the company, his team and about hiring the right people. He just thought that was the way it was done.

I sometimes wondered when I worked there how many good people had slipped through the net and never gone back to that second interview.

The only reason for being confrontational in an interview would be to test for a specific competency, and even then you would only do it if your behavioural interviewing were proving to be ineffective in uncovering that competency. But step carefully, because once someone’s guard has gone up as a result of you being confrontational, then their guard is up for the rest of the interview and you won't get anything useful and may well put the person off coming to work for you.

In terms of being polite, here are some other pointers. You would expect someone coming for an interview to be on time for that interview. The same applies to you. Be ready for the interview five minutes before the interview is due to start. If the candidate is already there, go and get them five minutes early. This acknowledges the fact to them that you know they were early, and they know that you were prepared.

2. Shut Up

Obviously I don't mean don't talk at all. However, as my mother used to say, "God gave you two ears and one mouth. Use them in that proportion." And certainly in an interview. You are there to find out about them, not to talk about yourself. At the end of the interview (as discussed), you will be talking to them about the job, the company and the future, and they will have the opportunity to ask you any questions they have. But for now, ask your question and then shut up. Nature abhors a vacuum, and the vacuum in conversation is always filled by the person who feels most uncomfortable. Let that not be you.

Sometimes it does feel awkward to leave a silence in an interview, but if you have asked a competency-based behavioural question, the person asked may well need a couple of seconds to mentally process that question and think of a relevant example to talk to you about. Don't rush in and spoil their thought process; allow them the time to respond.

3. Know Why You Are Asking

As mentioned earlier, it is important to know why you are asking each and every question. Don't ask questions that you think you “should” ask in an interview. If you don't write down the answer to a question, chances are it's because you're not interested in the answer, in which case - why ask the question in the first place? This also helps you not to fall foul of legalities. If you know you are asking the question because you are concerned that applicants may not be committed to the job and may leave to have children, for example, then by knowing what is motivating you to ask the question, you can stop yourself from asking what would be a discriminatory question which will fall foul of the law.

4. Know the Legals

It cannot be emphasised enough how very important it is that you keep yourself up to date with the legal aspects of hiring staff. This can be a minefield as employment law in the UK and probably elsewhere changes on a regular basis. As we speak, it is illegal in the UK to discriminate on grounds of gender, age, sex, sexual orientation disability, ethnicity, religion or belief, etc. It is very easy to fall foul of this without even trying.

For example, a client of ours with a large telesales operation interviewed someone for a job. The candidate was not suitable for a telesales role, as it was deemed his career history was not stable and that his communication skills were not at the high level required for this company. The candidate sued for racial discrimination in an interview. He felt that his race had something to do with the decision.

This could not have been further from the truth, as the client in question had one of the most diverse work forces it would be possible to imagine - with people from all races, religions, ages and sexualities in abundance.

But the candidate had been out of work for some time and was perhaps persuaded by some "no win no fee" lawyer that they had a case.

The company's lawyers felt that they had a very good chance of winning the case, as there were no serious grounds for the allegations, but the company decided to settle on the basis that it was many times cheaper to make the candidate a without-prejudice offer with no admission of liability than to go to court and incur the associated legal fees.

Firstly - it is time consuming to prepare for a tribunal and then to take the time out to attend. The company took the commercial decision that they would rather focus on the positive - running the business and making money - than focus on defending something of which they were not guilty that would have sapped many people's time and energy.

Good decision.

If by chance they lost (and who can ever be sure how tribunals will think on the day), it would have cost them more (in money and time and lost reputation). If (in all probability) they won, it would have cost them more (in money and time).

"Excuse me?" I hear you say. Why would it cost them more? Well, company lawyers do not work for free, and what do you think are the chances of securing several thousand pounds from an unemployed person? Plus, a tribunal will only award costs against a claimant if they feel strongly that the claimant brought the case maliciously. In the unlikely event that the tribunal allows a company to claim costs against the claimant, the fact remains - if they are unemployed and have no money, is the moral victory worth it?

Now do you want to know the killer fact about this case?

Wait for it...

The claimant was white and from Northern Ireland, which is part of the UK, and therefore you cannot use racial discrimination - or can you?

You can if you use your *cultural heritage* as a basis for the claim, apparently.

Are you scared now?

You should be!

The moral of that story is: ideally, consult an employment lawyer who has insurance backed products to offer their clients, (I can highly recommend David Walton at www.gorvins.com). Or at the very least join the Chamber of Commerce, the FSB, or another organisation that offers business support - and more importantly - legal insurance. If this company had been part of one of those organisations they could have pursued the case at no cost to themselves.

In terms of the time it would have taken and the cost, the decision to pay the applicant was the right commercial decision.

But it was the wrong moral decision. And everybody was very annoyed about it. So make sure you know the legals, including what you can and cannot ask in an interview.

For the most up-to-date version of this, go to the website http://www.thebookonrecruitment.com where you will find more on "the legals."

5. Take Notes

I've said it before and I will say it again. Take notes. Take notes. Take notes. If you are no good at taking notes, get somebody else to...take the notes.

Not only does this help you enormously in the rare and hopefully "never happening to you" scenario of an applicant trying to bring a case against you for discrimination in an interview. More importantly, unless you have a photographic memory, you *will* forget what was said in an interview. Unless you are planning to make a decision immediately after the interview and have no other candidates to compare against, you must take notes in order to remember everything that was said.

Also, taking notes is a good discipline to get into. As you become a more accomplished interviewer you will be able to see historically what kind of answers to your competency-based questions produced the most successful employees. And if at some point in the future you take on somebody who doesn't work out, you can go back and compare the notes on the interview with those from successful hires and see what was different.

You can also use what was said in the interview and what was promised – on both sides – in staff development and appraisals.

So take notes, and keep the notes, forever.

6. Say Cheese!

In the case where you may be interviewing multiple applicants – perhaps more than four - it can be very useful to take photographs.

It is 1000% easier to remember somebody from a photograph, even years later, than from a bunch of notes. It is a technique that I've used often over the years, and it's very useful, particularly if you have shared the interview process with one or more other interviewers and you are all sitting down to compare notes. If you have a photograph of the applicants that you're discussing you know everybody's discussing the same applicant.

One of the ways you can do that nowadays is to ask people to bring photo ID to the interview. It is your responsibility as an employer to ID check all applicants to ensure that they are legally entitled to work in the UK. (Did you know that?)

That is probably the best way of doing this and it makes it very easy to then remember the candidate afterwards. In the old days when I started recruiting, the way we did it was by using one of those instant cameras to take a picture in which the picture popped out at you a minute or so later. Of course, digital cameras are a little bit more efficient nowadays. We also used Morse code rather than telephones. I'm joking.

However, if you take photographs of people, you must ask them whether they are okay with that, so probably the simplest way to do it is to ask for a photo ID.

Chapter 8: Understanding What Can Go Wrong – The 10 Most Common Mistakes Other Businesses Make When Recruiting Staff (numbers 1 to 5)

Mistake Number 1 - Reacting and Rushing

For whatever reason, recruitment is normally a fairly unplanned event.

Someone has unexpectedly resigned, walked out or gone on long term sick. Perhaps they have decided not to return after maternity leave when you had expected them back. Perhaps they have asked if they can take early retirement or to work part time hours. Maybe they have just announced their pregnancy. Or maybe it's your business partner who has decided to sell up and ship out.

Alternatively, it could be that you have had a sudden unexpected upturn in business. A new product has gone better than expected, the market has suddenly seen increased demand for your product/service, or your new salesperson is bringing in more than anticipated revenues.

Whatever the reason, you didn't see it coming, didn't plan for it and weren't ready.

The natural reaction is “OMG (‘Oh My God,’ for the un text-initiated), I need someone fast."

This is the start of a chain of (fast moving) events often ending in the recruitment of someone so unsuitable that you couldn't have picked someone worse even if you had advertised for the opposite of what you were actually looking for.

I exaggerate...but only slightly.

The cost of getting recruitment wrong has been estimated at the low end at £5,000 per employee, but when accounting for all the costs (both real costs, such as time taken to select and recruit a replacement, and also opportunity costs, such as lost productivity), the cost of an employee for commercial organizations has been estimated at up to 150% of the employee’s remuneration package.

That is a huge amount of money and something often not considered in the rush to fill the empty seat.

So: when someone leaves, consider the cost and give yourself the time to consider all your options and plan your recruitment drive.

Mistake Number 2 - Moving Too Slowly

This may seem to contradict point 1 above, but here we are talking about once you have started your recruitment drive.

You absolutely should plan what needs to happen - and we will talk more about that in point 3 - but once you are ready to rock and roll, then don't delay.

Remember the three critical factors, two of which will apply to all prospective employees when they are looking for a new job.

Factor 1. They are currently unemployed.

Consider the reason why they are unemployed.

Just because they are unemployed, that doesn't mean there is anything wrong with them. Maybe their previous company has gone bump. Maybe they have been working abroad and just returned to the UK. Perhaps they are a recent graduate. Perhaps they have been caring for a sick family member. In rare cases, if candidates can afford to do so, they may prefer to leave their current job rather than keep taking time off to attend interviews (this normally would apply to very successful and sought-after candidates who are sure of their employability).

But be careful.

For someone to be made redundant once is bad luck. Twice is devastatingly bad luck. More than twice in a run might indicate that for them the word "redundant" is interchangeable with "sacked" or "left."

Check the references thoroughly.

Once you are satisfied that they are a good candidate for you, then remember this: all the time they are not employed, they are not earning a wage. If they were wealthy enough that this didn't matter to them then they wouldn't be looking for a job. They are probably out at other interviews that they have or have not told you about.

If your interview process is lengthy, you will probably lose them.

Some people in this situation take the view, “Well if they go, they go!” If you have doubts about them, or you find it easy to attract perfect staff, then go ahead and take this view. But if that is not the case, don't lose a potential star employee because you get too busy running the business or being side tracked, or because you are scared of making the wrong decision.

An ideal interview process should be no more than a week start to finish. Ideally, conduct it within the same calendar week.

If people have other options/job offers, they may be prepared to delay a day or two to come back for a second interview with you, if they really like the opportunity and the company at the first interview.

But give them a weekend in between to think about their other offers and you can kiss the candidate goodbye.

Factor 2. They are currently employed

This candidate also has options. They are not desperate and want to make sure they are making the right decision.

That doesn't mean you don't need to move fast.

They have a different set of problems.

How do they take time off for multiple interviews without raising suspicion at their current company? If they take too many odd days off on holiday and they have never done that before, they could have some awkward questions to answer.

Some candidates will book a few days' holiday and if you cannot fit them in when they have those days booked, then you may miss out.

Whatever their current employment status, good candidates don't stick around.

Though there may be more candidates in the market place at certain times (during a recession, for example), it doesn't mean that these are the best candidates - companies who make partial redundancies are not necessarily going to get rid of their best staff.

But believe me, the good ones are likely to have other options, whatever the state of the economy.

So don't make the mistake of thinking that you can drag out the interview process.

Factor 3. Candidates are Interviewing YOU!

It seems an obvious thing to say, but some employers still operate interviews from the perspective of benevolent parent, i.e. we are in control and we are trying to do you a favour by offering to give you a job.

They should wake up and smell the roses.

Unless you are the absolute top of your profession and have all the best people beating down your doors to come and work with you, do not make the mistake of forgetting to sell yourself, your company and their career prospects to your potential new hire.

And don't make the mistake of failing to look after people once they are with you. We have already looked at how expensive it is to make a recruitment mistake - there are the real costs (recruitment fees, advertising, wages before they are productive) - and the hidden costs (management time, training, lost productivity, low morale, lost customers).

Just as it is easier and cheaper to sell to existing customers than find new ones, it is easier and cheaper to focus on keeping existing staff than find new ones.

You should spend time on creating induction and training plans, making time for updates and appraisals, have an internal comms plan and involve staff in company plans.

Mistake Number 3 - Not Identifying What You Really Need

All too often when someone leaves a business they are replaced.

"So what's wrong with that?" I hear you say. "Isn't that what I am supposed to do?"

Not necessarily.

When someone leaves a business - and particularly if they have been with you for some time - it gives you time to consider what it is that you really need.

Businesses change.

The needs of the business change. The person you took on four years ago to do a bit of admin, bookkeeping and generally run the office for you has grown to be the person who does the payroll, does the inbound sales and looks after the marketing.

Maybe the reason they are leaving is that their salary has failed to keep pace with their growing job responsibilities.

(Actually, that is *not* the number one reason people leave their jobs - if you want to know what that is, go to our website www.thebookonrecruitment.com and download our report: "The Five Most Common Reasons People Leave Their Job and What To Do About It".)

What will be true is this: the person you employed four years ago at £15,000 is *not* the person that is leaving today.

Do you need to replace that person with the person who walked in four years ago, or the person who walked out today?

Or do you need something different?

Perhaps it is time to outsource the finance work, or get an office junior and employ a dedicated sales and marketing person? Perhaps you should outsource the sales and marketing and bring in an FD? Or perhaps you should outsource the finance *and* marketing and bring in an Office Manager/PA?

See what I mean?

You now have options.

Don't rush into looking for a replica of the person who left until you have determined what exactly the business needs in terms of skills and experience going forward.

Oh - and another thought.

If you *do* decide to replace the person who left, do remember you are not going to get them for the salary you were paying them when they started, *or* when they left.

Most people who leave a business move to another business doing more or less the *same* job but for more money (and no, that is still not the Number One reason people leave a business).

Be realistic in your expectations.

If you can only afford the person who joined four years ago then you may need to lower your expectations back down to the skills you employed at that time.

On the other hand if you know you *need* all the skills your "leaver" had acquired in the last four years, then bite the bullet - you are probably going to have to pay more.

Mistake Number 4 - Delegating to Someone Who Doesn't Have the Skills

Oh boy! This is an easy one to do.

You don't have the time to deal with this recruitment need.

You are far too busy running your business/your division. You know recruitment is a time consuming nightmare, and in times of recession even more so - and you will probably end up with hundreds of CV's sitting on your desk.

So you delegate.

You have an ambitious team leader who wants to help out.

Or worse - you dump the job on someone you think has the time to do it.

But do they have the experience?

Have another think about the cost of getting it wrong. Now - does it still seem as attractive an option to delegate out?

This is *your* business, after all.

It is your revenue, your profits, your customers, your other staff - who will be affected if it goes wrong.

Still think you should delegate it?

Okay - then make sure the person you delegate it to has the experience, knowledge and the motivation to do a good job.

If you don't have that person internally then ask for some recommendations of a reputable agency who can take all the time consuming stuff away from you and give you a guarantee on the placement in case it goes wrong.

Mistake Number 5 - Not Involving Everyone Who Needs to Buy In

If you are an owner-managed business, or the senior partner in a business, or in charge of your own division or department of a larger business, you may not be used to involving anyone else in the process.

Or you may involve your business partner or your HR person (if you have one).

That is fine and absolutely right - but perhaps there are other people who should also be involved.

As you grow your business, it will grow faster and happier if your staff get along.

That doesn't mean they need to be best friends or socialise together after work, but it does mean they need to not hate each other.

There needs to be synergy in their beliefs and values.

There have been countless examples of existing staff sabotaging new staff - often subconsciously - because they feel threatened or don't understand what the role of the new person is and why it is important for the business.

Equally, there are countless other examples of new people coming into a business and failing to fit in, causing morale problems and ultimately leaving.

Cultural fit is a very important part of the interview process and unless you are 100 % sure of your ability to get it right every time (and I would argue even if you are), getting key staff involved in some way in the process can only have positive outcomes.

Even if you have made your mind up to take someone on, getting the person who will sit next to them involved can have many benefits.

If you trust your employee, you can leave the room.

The prospective employee can then ask what they like about working at the company and get a colleague eye view of the opportunity. The existing member of staff feels their views are important and they feel valued. They may have a different perspective than you and pick up on something you missed, as possibly the new employee may be more open with them.

They may (and hopefully will, most of the time) agree with your decision and give you more confidence about hiring - or rejecting - that particular applicant.

The one thing you must do before involving a colleague in an interview is explain very clearly why you are hiring and the benefit to the existing employee of the hire, and of their involvement in the hiring process. Then ensure you explain very clearly what you want them to do/not do in the meeting.

This is equally true and even more important if you are involving a business partner in the process. If you don't involve them or clearly agree between you what your various roles are in the recruitment process and who will make the decision/how the decision will be made, then you risk not only looking unprofessional but failing to come to an agreement on the hire.

In addition, if you have a company social coming up, it is a good idea to invite your prospective employee along. In a larger organisation you might want to hold assessment centres where you can observe candidates reacting to other people in "real life" situations. This is a much larger subject; for a report on the benefits of assessment centres go to www.thebookonrecruitment.com and download the report on running assessment centres.

In the absence of an assessment centre, inviting the candidate out for dinner or drinks can be very revealing. You will often get to see more of the real them and sometimes the parts of them that they would rather you didn't see.

Okay. We are gathering speed and in the next chapter we will look at Mistake Number 6 - and this one is a KILLER...

Chapter 9 - Understanding What Can Go Wrong: The 10 Most Common Mistakes Other Businesses Make When Recruiting Staff (numbers 6 to 10)

Mistake Number 6 - Not Knowing the Legals

This is a scary one. It is hard enough for someone who is a full time HR or Recruitment Specialist to keep up with the ever-changing flow of legals, never mind someone whose job is running a business.

But let me make it really clear: you have to. Otherwise you leave yourself wide open for all kinds of trouble.

It is so easy to get it wrong in all sorts of ways re the legalities of employing staff. Employment law seems to change almost weekly, and that's without the constant interference from Brussels.

At the time of writing there have been recent changes not everyone is aware of and more to come - and I don't see that constant change ending any time soon.

Recent examples of companies acting unintentionally illegally/being unaware of things they need to know include the following:

1. Not knowing the minimum wage - do you know what it is? What about for 16 - 18 year olds? What about for a 20 year old?

2. Do you check if people have the proper work permit, or even if they need them? Do you know which countries they apply to?

3. Do you know the very strict guidelines on self-employed people? You could end up with a big tax and NI bill in the case of many "self-employed" candidates.

4. What about commission-only salespeople? Did you know that under most circumstances that is unlawful? There are very strict rules as to who you can pay a commission-only structure to.

5. At what age can you make people retire? You might be surprised at the answer to that.

6. Why can you not ask for a degree from a specific university?

7. What medical questions are you allowed to ask?

8. Is there ever a case where you can be gender specific in a recruitment drive? (The answer is a surprise to most people.)

I don't propose to answer these questions here because by the time you read them the rules may have changed again. If you would like the current answers to these questions go to: www.thebookonrecruitment.com and go to our "ask David" section, where you will find the most current answers.

These are just some of the literally *hundreds* and possibly *thousands* of things you need to be aware of when you recruit.

We have already looked at two very scary examples earlier in the book – the hairdresser and the telesales applicant. Let's look at one more...

There was the case of Tahir Hussain, who failed to get an interview for a job as a car salesperson at a Yorkshire garage, and who subsequently took the garage to an Employment Tribunal claiming race discrimination. He did this on the basis that he also submitted an identical CV to that same garage, but replaced his own name on the CV with the name of a fictitious white female. That fictitious white female secured an interview! Mr Hussain won his case against the garage, in addition to four further cases against other businesses who did exactly the same thing, and he settled a further four cases brought on the same grounds, cashing in to the tune of some £25,000.

Now are you scared?

Mistake Number 7 - The Incorrect Use of Gut Feeling

Okay: let's get one thing straight up front.

I am *not* proposing that you ignore your gut. Quite the opposite - you must listen to it!

But you must also question it and search for evidence to support it. And if the evidence you find tells you something else, then you must give that serious thought and act accordingly. This is what makes a great hiring decision.

Before you take issue with me on that point, please answer the following questions honestly.

Do you use gut feeling when hiring staff? Have you - or anyone you know - ever hired someone who didn't work out?

If the answer to the above is, "No, Carole, I do use gut feeling, I have no interview process, and I have never made a poor hiring decision," then congratulations.

You probably don't need this book - no hang on - you probably still do, and let me tell you why.

Even if your gut feelings are impeccable, if you want to grow your business then one day you will have to delegate some interviewing/hiring responsibilities to someone else.

When that day comes, let me ask you this question: How does someone else replicate your gut feeling?

Answer:

They can't.

Therefore, you need a process that you can follow, one you can teach your future managers, a system that can identify what it is about your gut feeling that works and what doesn't.

Gut feeling, by the way, is not some mystical power that only a few people possess. It is the accumulation of all your experiences and knowledge that is so deeply ingrained in you that you don't consciously access it - but it makes itself known as gut feeling.

With some work, you can unravel this and understand what your gut feeling is telling you and why. At that level of self knowledge you can really leverage your gut feeling - but that is a topic for another day.

Like it or not, without a process, the people that managers/business owners hire are generally "mini me's." That might or might not be what the role requires.

If your main skills are finance and detail, for example, and you are trying to hire a salesperson on gut feeling with no process, what do you think is likely to happen?

You got it - the salesperson can't sell and your great plans of growing the business come to nothing.

The same can work the other way around - you are a great salesperson - in fact you are *the* chief salesperson in your business. You need to hire an office manager - someone to make sure the necessary supplies, people, resources are where they need to be so that the machine of your business works once you have brought in the sales.

You hire another you - and that works for a while - but eventually the system breaks down because the things you thought were being done in the background were being ignored because the people person you hired was spending all their time talking to people (suppliers, clients, staff) and not enough time creating and operating the systems in your business.

There are six main evaluation mistakes people can make when hiring: Halo, Horns, Primacy, Similarity, Stereotyping and Lack of Evidence (to back up or challenge their gut feelings).

I am not going to go into all of these, but let's pick on the first two to make a point of when and where gut feeling can be useful or harmful. You can find information on the other four by going to www.thebookonrecruitment.com and looking for the report on the six most common evaluation mistakes.

The Halo effect - This is where - at some point in the interview - the interviewee says something with which you so totally agree or which so excites you that you make your mind up at that point that they are the person you want and you will ultimately be offering them the job.

What then happens is that for the rest of the interview your subconscious is looking for "evidence" that you are right. Everything that person says from that point on is interpreted in a positive light and any potentially worrying or concerning comments will either be ignored or excused.

This happened to me many years ago, and it was after I had already created the "More Than a Gut Feeling" Interview process that we now share with clients.

I really should have known better, but - like the builder who ignores his own house DIY - I thought my instincts for recruiting the right people were so good after many years and literally thousands of interviews (for ourselves and for our clients) that I could afford to ignore my own process.

What happened is this:

I taught my team leaders to use the "More Than a Gut Feeling" process. They were keen to practice their new skills. They interviewed a candidate who wanted to work for us. I also interviewed him, and my (temporary) boss - who hadn't done the training - also interviewed him.

My boss and I liked him, but my two team leaders were uncertain. I made the assumption that as it was their first run through, they may not have followed the process. I had also noted something in the interview that would normally have been a concern - but I liked the candidate. More than that - he had said something in the interview regarding his previous successes - which immediately exercised the Halo Effect on me.

And I didn't even recognise it when it happened.

My boss liked him a lot, I trusted his judgement and my own, and we made the decision to hire him.

It was a terrible decision.

He was an immediate starter, so he came to work the next day, before we had taken up references. By the time we obtained references a couple of weeks later it was already apparent that the candidate had not done some of the things he had claimed to do and was not the right person for the role.

We had to let him go.

From a business point of view, we failed quickly (always a good rule to follow); we didn't drag things out and therefore our financial exposure was minimised.

But the lesson was a hard one. I apologised to my team leaders for underestimating their ability to implement our system, congratulated them for remaining objective despite their initially warm feelings about the candidate, and allowed them free rein in the replacement recruitment drive, which they conducted very successfully.

It was a great example to the team - that the system works, if you let it! And it made the point to me that however good your gut feelings are, if you don't follow the system, you are in danger of getting it wrong.

You can probably guess at the Horns Effect?

This is Halo in reverse.

The Horns Effect - This is where a candidate says or does something in the interview which turns the interviewer off, and after that point in the interview, every piece of evidence points to the fact that you shouldn't hire this person. Any evidence that you should is conveniently overlooked or explained away. This following illustrates this perfectly.

When I worked as Regional Manager for one of the UK's largest IT recruitment companies, we hired many staff.

All of them had no experience in recruitment as we preferred to train our own, and each Director had a very clear vision of what they wanted in a new recruit.

I interviewed a girl who was straight out of Uni. She won't mind me saying she did not have the best business suit in the world, in fact I don't think she had a business suit at that time and maybe wasn't as polished as she could have been.

This was not a problem in my mind. You can buy a suit. Someone can give you grooming tips and when you start to earn money you can improve your wardrobe and your haircut.

What she did have was intelligence, drive, tenacity, grit and problem solving skills.

I loved her and my MD - who happened to be in my office that day - said she would like to interview her. So she did.

She came out of the interview and said she was a definite no – the reason being she had a belly button ring.

Well, in my opinion, once we had this girl earning the money to buy proper business suits, no one was going to see her belly button!

I hired her. She started her career as my resourcer, at which she was brilliant, later moved to consultant and later opened her own financial recruitment business.

Beware those horns!

Mistake Number 8 – So Easy to Do: Not Selling the Opportunity

What's the purpose of the interview?

If someone asked me that question I would probably say something like, "Well Carole, the purpose of the interview is for me to find the best possible person for my new role. I want to find out all about them and make sure that they fit all the criteria I am looking for and if they are going to be able to do the job."

That's the right answer...isn't it?

Well, kind of.

Let me ask the question again.

What's the purpose of the interview, both for you and for the prospective employee?

Does that change your answer?

Most people when interviewing fall into a trap (present company excluded of course!). The trap they fall into is in thinking that they are in control of the interview – which leads them into making the 8th Biggest Mistake.

The candidate is looking for a job - they have come for the interview - so they must want the job, right?

WRONG.

The candidate is interested in finding out if this is the right job for them. At best - if you have used a great agency (see point 9 in the series) - then they should be very interested. They should already feel that it is probably the job for them

Most candidates, though, are anywhere from mildly interested to very interested, but in 99% of cases they have not decided *this* is the job for them. See the difference?

So - the 8th most common mistake employers make is *not* selling the job, the company and the future to the candidate.

So you decide to sell the opportunity to the candidate.

But when is the best time to do that, and how?

Many companies would do it right at the beginning of the interview - that would raise interest levels in the applicant, wouldn't it?

Not necessarily.

At the beginning of the interview the candidate has a lot going on in their mind. They are probably nervous and they are desperately trying to remember all the things they want to say to you. They may not be paying the highest amount of attention to the blurb about the role. Or as already discussed, they might listen and change the answers to your questions due to the clues you have given them in your explanations of the job.

Also - how do you know at this stage what to tell them?

Have you heard the one about the cruise missile and Dad's Army?

No, it's not the beginning of a stand up comic act. It's a metaphor. In World War 2 when the Luftwaffe came over, the home guard (as portrayed in the wonderful comedy "Dad's Army") would get the guns out and fire - pretty blindly - into the sky until their bullets ran out in the hope that they would hit something. In my grandfather's case, what they hit was the Home Guard Building, and some trees, but they didn't actually hit an enemy plane (bless them for trying!).

Compare that to the cruise missiles in the first Gulf War. One missile would be fired and it would track and take out the SCUD missile the other side had fired.

The moral of that story in relation to interviewing is this: find out (ideally from your agency beforehand) what the main motivations of the interviewee are. What are they interested in?

Do they want money? Career progression? Is it training that really turns them on? Perhaps it is autonomy? Maybe they are really sociable and want to work somewhere with a strong social culture.

Whatever it is - if you know - you can spend more time talking about this - giving the detail that will enable the candidate to really feel and imagine themselves in the role.

And do this at the end - after they have asked all their questions and answered yours. That way they are listening to you, and the "why they should want the job" is the freshest thing in their mind when they leave.

In that way, you have the best possible chance of standing out amongst the other offers that may come their way.

Try it!

The 9th Most Common Mistake – Thinking You Can or Should Do Everything

I am going to share with you some thoughts about agencies.

The 9th most common mistake employers make is not using a brilliant agency - or conversely - using a not brilliant one.

You are an expert in what you do.

Whether you run your own company or work for someone else. Whether you are an engineer, an accountant, a solicitor or a salesman. Whatever your skill set - compared to most people - you are an expert.

So let me pose a question...

If you are not an accountant - would you do your own company accounts?
If you are not a barrister - would you defend yourself in court?
If you are not an engineer - would you design your own air conditioning system?

Obviously not. That would be crazy!

So - why are you doing your own recruitment if you are not an expert in recruitment?
Surely, hiring staff is *the* most important thing a business owner can ever do.

We discussed earlier how much hiring the wrong person can cost a business. In extreme circumstances it can close a business down.

So - unless you are totally cash strapped and time rich (in which case I would suggest you think twice about recruiting - unless it is for a top class salesperson) - why would you not use a specialist?

Like any field in life there are good ones and bad ones - and perhaps the reputation the industry has is not totally undeserved.

However, a brilliant recruiter can pay for themselves twentyfold in time saved for you, and in cash made for the business.

A brilliant recruiter will take the time to get to know your business inside and out; will understand your plans and vision for the company and be able to present interesting candidates to you when they arise (not just when you are under pressure to recruit)

They can keep you advised of changes to employment law and will always work with you and share the risk with you in any hiring situation.

So - how do you fight your way through the myriad of agencies all promising the same thing?

First rule of business: if something looks too good to be true, it probably is. Equally, if something looks cheap, it probably is. Don't take the cheapest option unless it is also the best option.

This is so important - forgive me for repeating it.

DO NOT take the cheapest option unless it is also the best option.

Referral is the cheapest option - but only take on someone from referral if they are also the perfect candidate for your business. It will cost you more in the long run if they are not. If you can't find anyone suitable from referral, then ask for referrals to a quality recruiter.

And if that doesn't produce the goods, look for a recruiter that is a member of the Chamber of Commerce or other body (it doesn't guarantee anything, but it means they are bothered enough to want to participate in the local economy). And look for an agency where the individuals (not the agency) are REC qualified.

The REC (Recruitment Employment Confederation) is the industry body in the UK. You can buy membership to this organisation as you can to many industry bodies, and to be fair, it doesn't mean that much to you as a client.

An agency doesn't have to be part of REC to operate and many are not, including some national and household names. It is an industry body - existing largely like any industry body - for the benefit of its members.

The REC badge *can* benefit you though.

Want to know how?

Look for a firm where the individual consultants are REC qualified. That means they have had to undertake a year's study (at least) in four areas - the Law, the Marketplace, Dealing with Clients and Understanding and Interviewing Candidates.

Then they have to pass an exam in those subjects. That means a little more than just having the badge. So look for an agency where the consultants *and* the owner are REC qualified.
Consider also the following criteria: Does the consultant offer to visit you so that they understand your environment? How much time do they spend asking questions about the role, the company, the future plans, the team? How do they interview their candidates? How much detail do they go into? How are their consultants targeted? What guarantees do they offer?

Remember - recruitment is in many cases a high-pressure sales environment where activity levels are often monitored closely. That's not a bad thing in itself, but it can lead to more junior consultants sending unsuitable candidates to hit their interview targets for the week.

On the other hand, an agency will have access to far more candidates than you will; they will generally have accounts with one or more of the major job boards, and have a database full of candidates before they have to place an advert.

In addition, they should be expert in other methods of finding candidates which the average business will have neither the time, the resources, or the knowledge to be able to utilise.

The right agency can save you huge amounts of time in the screening process. Some will conduct first interviews for you, some may be able to reference and background check candidates, some may be able to compose an advertising campaign for you and negotiate rates with the media, and some will be able to advise you on interviewing techniques.

All good agencies should be able to give you more of an insight into the candidate than you would otherwise get by just interviewing; candidates will often be more open with their agency than with a potential employer.
And some of the best candidates would never apply direct for anything, will always go through an agency because they haven't the time in their busy lives to deal with the application process for multiple opportunities. They would rather apply once and then get their agency to do all the hard work.

Most agencies will also guarantee your new recruit for a period of time, and of course, you don't have to pay anything until your new person has started working with you.

So there really is no risk from using (the right) agency, and much to gain.

Try claiming your money back from a newspaper or Internet job board that you have paid to advertise with if your new recruit leaves after several weeks.

Not a chance!

Mistake Number 10 – Hiring Only on Skills

This is easy to do and totally understandable. After all - it is vital that you get the person with the right skills to do the jobs, isn't it?
That would be obvious...right?

Well, not necessarily.

I will agree - in certain circumstances - it is essential that the skills are bang on. After all, no one would want their brain surgery carried out by someone who is not a qualified brain surgeon. But in many roles the skills are actually not as important as the core competencies of the individual.

After all, skills, by definition, are things which have been acquired/taught/learnt. Therefore you can teach skills and they can be learnt. This is not the difficult bit (in most cases - brain or other surgery excepted!).

What cannot be taught and is generally either there or it is not there, are values and core competencies. How do you teach a salesperson to be "driven" or an accountant to love detail?

You really can't.

There has to be a tendency there already - and if there is, then the competency can be developed - but some things are just beyond some people whilst for others they are as easy as falling off a log.

Take me for example.

You could probably - with a lot of effort on your part and on mine - teach me how to write a short computer programme (very short!). Even though I have no interest in it, writing simple code is a skill which can be learned. However, you could never teach me to quit, because I am not a quitter, no matter how hopeless the outcome may look.

Neither could you teach someone to be charismatic, motivated or positive. You *must* hire on attitudes/competencies and values. Even if you feel it essential to hire on skills, you must *not* hire *only* on skills.

So we are back to the message about hiring on competencies. I apologise for belabouring the point – actually, no I don't. This is the most important message in the book.

A company I once worked with once had a huge problem with staff turnover.

After much research and analysis it came down to poor hiring, and particularly the hiring of the same spec person for the multiple sales teams. But that sound logical doesn't it? Possibly - but it was still wrong. Each team is a micro-culture, and in a larger company, whilst there may be a "company" culture, there is also a team culture.

So it is critical to identify what these core competencies are and once they are identified that you use the behavioural interviewing techniques discussed to bring out the evidence you are looking for in the interview.

Not doing this part of the process is probably the single most important reason why many employers get hiring the right staff so very wrong.

You can't get a size twelve foot into a size six shoe except by chopping the toes off.

Ouch - sorry about that nasty analogy - but it is absolutely valid.

If you don't know you have a "size twelve foot" and you hire it, then it/they won't fit and will leave pretty quickly, causing much mayhem along the way and telling everyone they know about your awful little size six shoe and how they were conned into trying it on.

Or you (or they) will chop off the toes and try to fit. Only that doesn't work out either in the long run, and meanwhile, by trying to fit into something that isn't right, their confidence is eaten away on a daily basis and you don't get the performance you were expecting but can't understand why.

Competency-based interviewing is not just about asking a few situational questions; it is core to the success of the process and the competencies must align with yours, with the company's and with the vision of the future.

Big subject - too big to go into in any more depth in this book.

My suggestion is to get some help with this one. It is so easy to get it wrong, but so important to get it right.

That's the last of "The 10 Most Common Mistakes Most Employers Make when Hiring Staff and How to Avoid Them."

There are others. "What?" I hear you say. "There are more than ten things that could go wrong?"

Well, yes, but that's for another time!

For now, thank you for reading this far and I hope you have enjoyed and have gotten something out of it.

If even one part of the ten subjects covered resonated with you or just made you stop and think of something that you could use in your process, then I will be really happy. I would be happy to hear about your experiences and any feedback you may have is always appreciated. Please go to the website www.thebookonrecruitment.com/feedback or email me on mailto:carole@thebookonrecruitment.com.

Chapter 10 - A Foolproof Method for Deciding, or "Deciding for Dummies"

So we're nearly there.

We've looked at the following:

- Why you should have a proper recruitment process
- How to create the perfect job spec and the perfect person spec
- How to find the candidates that you need
- The magic 5 to 8: identifying the competencies
- Questioning the criteria: how to devise behavioural interviewing questions
- 10-step process: planning a successful interview
- Questioning dos and don'ts: tips from the experts
- Understanding what can go wrong: the 10 most common mistakes 1 – 5
- The 10 most common mistakes: 6– 10

So what's left?

The only thing we have to do now is create a process for evaluation.

This is quite straightforward to do as long as you have taken copious notes during the interview as I have mentioned on several occasions. The first thing to do is to go to the URL www.thebookonrecruitment.com and download the evaluation chart.

As you will see from the chart, the first column is where you would put the criteria. In the next column you would put the behaviour. In the example you have downloaded the criteria is "resilience" and the two behaviours are "maintaining personal effectiveness despite pressure" and "dealing with rejection."

The chart gives you an opportunity to note down any positive – or negative - evidence, by which I mean any evidence which would suggest that the person does *not* display the behaviour you are looking for and therefore may not have competency you require. You should make brief notes in that column to remind you what that evidence is.

If there is no evidence either negative or positive of that behaviour, then please note that there are two potential reasons for no evidence. The first is that there are genuinely no examples of the person exhibiting this behaviour. Once you have been interviewing in this way for some time and are confident with your skills in competency-based behavioural interviewing, then no evidence in this column would indeed suggest that they do not have any examples of those behaviours and therefore do not have competency you are looking for. In this case, it's definitely not the person for you.

As we have discussed already, competencies are the core requirements; they are not trainable, and they are not negotiable. If you have identified the competencies correctly, then that is what you need for that role. If you look at the evaluation sheet and there is no evidence on one of the competencies, you should not take on that person. It is as simple as that. If you decide that actually you still want to take on that person, then either you are saying that item is not a core competency, in which case remove it from future recruitment drives, or you are risking making a poor hiring decision. Your call!

The other reason why there would be a tick in the "no evidence" box - and this is much more common in your first few times of doing competency-based behavioural interviewing - is that your skills as an interviewer need to be developed. It may well be that this person does have examples they could have brought to the table, but perhaps your questions didn't uncover them.

This may be an area that you could go over again in a second interview. If everything else on the evaluation sheet looked positive and there was one area with no evidence and you felt that perhaps that has occurred because you are new to this type of interviewing, then you could use that as something to re-evaluate in a second interview.

You then have three columns for positive evidence. They should be self-explanatory. In those columns you would make brief notes of the positive evidence you have of those behaviours to remind yourself what to discuss with your fellow interviewers.

The final column says "acceptable?". In this column you can either put yes, maybe, or no. I would suggest it is better to put in a numeric value. So, for example, if you had two pieces of positive evidence and one piece of negative evidence, that would give you a numeric value of one. Ideally, you want a numeric value of two in order to be happy that the person displays the behaviour you are looking for. Since you will have a minimum of two behaviours for each competency, you are looking for a numeric score of four or more for each competency.

On the basis you are looking for - in this example, five competencies - your end score needs to be twenty. Not nineteen or eighteen: twenty is the minimum score for an interview of five competencies.

How easy is that?

As long as you have:

- taken enough notes,
- identified the core competencies,

- drilled down to the correct behaviours that will illustrate the competencies,
- framed past tense based behavioural questions to identify these competencies...

...then filling in the evaluation chart is a simple process. And your decision is therefore very easy.

Phew! That's it. You now have the tools you require to go off and recruit your next member of staff.

But before you do, lets recap...

Conclusion

Can I guarantee that by using this system, you will never make another recruitment mistake?

Of course not.

Employees are human beings. Human beings are fundamentally unpredictable. As they say, "Shit happens." Like the lady in her twenties who was diagnosed with cancer. There are underlying medical conditions and underlying psychological conditions which can change people almost overnight.

When interviewing, you might not be on top form; maybe you didn't get enough sleep the night before, or maybe you're slightly distracted by the pressures of business. Perhaps the candidate does a particularly bad interview where on another day they could have secured the job, or did an amazing interview which was above their true competency level.

What I can tell you is that using any process will be better than using no process at all. And that using this process has been proven on thousands of occasions to vastly improve the success rate of hiring the right people.

As a small business owner, recruiting the right staff is the most important thing you can do. But I'll bet my bottom dollar that unless you have worked for a FTSE 100 company, no one has ever trained you how to do this most vital activity.

I know, because you are reading this book, that you appreciate how important recruitment is to you and your business. I hope that you now feel more confident in your ability to conduct this process with a higher degree of success. And I thank you very much for making this investment of your time into reading *The Book on Recruitment* and acquiring the skills that will make you successful as a recruiter.

You now have the basics of the entire recruitment process.

You know that you need to start with the **company's vision and values**, its brand and what it stands for. Hopefully, that exercise will help you not only with your recruitment, but also with your marketing and PR, with your exit strategy, and with all parts of your business. But it should be fundamental to your recruitment, staff management and staff development.

You know how to create **a person spec and a job spec**. You know how and where to find potential candidates.

You know the basics of pulling together recruitment advertising and how to use an agency should you choose to do so and how to get the most out of the relationship.

Most importantly, you know **how to identify the key criteria, the key competencies** that the person doing that specific role within your team or company will need and you know how to identify the behaviours and then frame **the behavioural questions** will help you uncover whether interviewees possess those competencies.

You also know **how to structure an interview** and the basic do's and don'ts of interviewing.

And you know the ten most common mistakes that other businesses make when hiring staff and how to avoid them.

Crucially, you know how to simply and **objectively identify and evaluate your interviews** and decide who, if any, of the people you interviewed are right for this role.

Bonus Material

As a thank you for reading this book and for caring enough to put in place a proper recruitment process for your business, I would like to give you some stuff for free. Some of this has been mentioned during the course of the book but to re-cap, go to the website www.thebookonrecruitment.com and enter the code BOR1 when prompted

You can download a variety of forms from the job spec, the person spec, evaluation form, the funnel and SOARE sheet and various ad templates. You can download the list of competencies, a list of behaviours relating to those competencies, and a variety of behavioural questions. You can access the tick sheet for the 10 steps to interview success process. And you can download the 10 most common mistakes as a PDF or as a 10-day e-mail series.

You can also access up-to-date legal information and in addition an extra special report, "14 Tips from Industry Experts to Guarantee Your Recruitment Success".

Once you've registered on the website, you can continue to access all the freebies that will be available and we will keep you informed of our "more than a gut feeling" interview training seminars, and other events which will be happening around the country or the world.

Afterword

If you enjoyed this book then look out for my next book, which will be part two of the book on recruitment - *From Hired to Fired. What Goes Wrong in Most Small Businesses after Hiring Staff and How to Avoid It.*

Thank you once again for spending the time to read the book all the way to the end. That already puts you in the top 10% of small business owners, most of whom buy business books with the best of intentions and five years later those books are still on the shelves unread. Well done.

Till next time,

Carole

26227908R00090

Printed in Great Britain
by Amazon